Keynotes in Criminology and Criminal Justice Series

WHITE-COLLAR AND CORPORATE CRIME

D0165450

Gilbert Geis, Ph.D.
University of California, Irvine

New York   Oxford
OXFORD UNIVERSITY PRESS

Oxford University Press is a department of the University of Oxford.
It furthers the University's objective of excellence in research,
scholarship, and education by publishing worldwide.

Oxford   New York
Auckland   Cape Town   Dar es Salaam   Hong Kong   Karachi
Kuala Lumpur   Madrid   Melbourne   Mexico City   Nairobi
New Delhi   Shanghai   Taipei   Toronto

With offices in
Argentina   Austria   Brazil   Chile   Czech Republic   France   Greece
Guatemala   Hungary   Italy   Japan   Poland   Portugal   Singapore
South Korea   Switzerland   Thailand   Turkey   Ukraine   Vietnam

For titles covered by Section 112 of the US Higher Education
Opportunity Act, please visit www.oup.com/us/he for the
latest information about pricing and alternate formats.

Published by Oxford University Press
198 Madison Avenue, New York, New York 10016
http://www.oup.com

CIP data is on file at the Library of Congress.

ISBN: 978-0-19-021928-4

Printing number: 9 8 7 6 5 4 3 2 1

Printed in the United States of America
on acid-free paper

Keynotes in Criminology and Criminal Justice Series

WHITE-COLLAR AND CORPORATE CRIME

CONTENTS

To Dolores and in memory of Robley Geis and for Joe Wells and the Association of Certified Fraud Examiners

---

ACKNOWLEDGMENTS

The most pleasant and gratifying part of my academic life has been the opportunity to form friendships and exchange ideas with scholars and practitioners in the United States and throughout the world who share my interest in and concerns about white-collar and corporate crime. We read each other's work, exchange reprints, criticize, and praise. We come together intermittently at conferences and workshops, getting to meet spouses and children, brag, and complain. It seems after a while that we become part of an extended family that is bound together by a common focus and shared knowledge and memories.

I will not identify all these colleagues individually. They make up a goodly part of the roster of names in the Index, and without their scholarly research and theorizing, this book would not have been possible. I thank them collectively.

When I first began to write about white-collar crime, about half a century ago, it was a lonesome enterprise, particularly when Senator Joseph McCarthy and his witch-hunting committee defined anything that challenged the power elite as subversive. When the Associated Press carried a story about what at the time would have been regarded by McCarthy as my un-American views, I collected a considerable pile of abusive mail from around the country suggesting, among the more polite proposals, that I go back to Russia—where I had never been. Today, there is a considerable corps of people who focus on white-collar crime, and their contributions and intellectual companionship are invaluable.

Teaching jobs were few and far between when I went on the market in 1952, and I was delighted to be hired at the University of Oklahoma, sight unseen (which may well have been for the best), while I was writing my dissertation in Norway. I was assigned to teach criminology, though I had never had a criminology course as a graduate or undergraduate student. I frantically read material, often the night before class, and regurgitated what I had learned. It was then that I encountered Edwin Sutherland's *White Collar Crime*, and it became something of a lodestar for me. For one thing, I had been brought up amidst an iconoclastic student body and teaching staff as part of the first graduating class at the Bronx High School of Science. For another, I sensed that I preferred to focus on the abuse of power rather than the abuse of the powerless.

This book owes its birth most particularly to the midwife efforts of Henry Pontell, a longtime colleague and friend, who oversees the series in which the book appears, and to Frank Mortimer, a considerate and innovative publishing colleague. I also want to express my appreciation to an array of persons who in different ways have made this book possible and my life better: Kimley Do and Mike Agopian, Miho Akada, Virginia and Arnie Binder, Valerie and John Braithwaite, Nora and Chris Brown, Lesley and Ivan Bunn, Fred Caron, Jacque Carter, Debby Newquist and Joe DiMento, Warren Enst, Pete Fischler, Connie Franco, Bill Frohlich, Bronwyn Stuart and Peter Grabosky, Julianne Ohlander and Paul Jesilow, Don Maniguele, Shampa and Sanjoy Mazumdar, Steve Reynard, Larry Salinger, Dale Sechrest, David Shichor, Mary Dodge and Jere Stahl, Ken Tokash, Ralph Venuto, Judy and Joe Wells, and Richard Wright.

As for family members, children and their children, I will only indicate that they are precious to me, the bedrock of my existence.

At the University of California, Irvine, I owe a debt of gratitude to Diane Christianson and Patty Edwards, and to the Interlibrary Loan and Document Delivery Service people who so efficiently keep me in business: Pamela S. La Zar, Linda Weinberger, Dianna Sahhar, and Gerry Lopez.

Keynotes in Criminology and Criminal Justice Series

This Series is designed to provide essential knowledge on important contemporary matters of crime, law, and justice to a broad audience of readers including students, educators, researchers, and practitioners alike, and in a format that is not only authoritative, but highly engaging, and concise. Nationally and internationally respected scholars share their knowledge and unique insights in comprehensive surveys and penetrating analyses of a variety of major contemporary issues central to the study of criminology, criminal justice, and social justice more generally. Forthcoming and planned Series books cover such areas as electronic crime, race, crime and justice, white-collar and corporate crime, violence in international perspective, gender and crime, gangs, mass incarceration, police and surveillance, financial fraud, and critical criminology.

I invite you to examine the Series and see how these readable, affordable, topical, and highly informative books can be used to help educate a new generation of students in understanding the social realities surrounding crime and justice in both domestic and global perspective.

Henry N. Pontell, Editor
Keynotes in Criminology and Criminal Justice Series
Distinguished Professor, John Jay College of Criminal Justice, CUNY
Professor Emeritus, University of California, Irvine

ABOUT THE AUTHOR

Gilbert Geis was professor emeritus, Department of Criminology, Law and Society at the University of California, Irvine. He received his Ph.D. in sociology at the University of Wisconsin and taught at the University of Oklahoma, and California State University, Los Angeles, before coming to Irvine in 1971. He was a visiting professor at SUNY Albany, Penn State, and John Jay College, and he received Fulbright grants for research work in Norway, Portugal, and Australia. He has more than 500 professional publications—books, book chapters, and articles. He is a former president of the American Society of Criminology and recipient of its Edwin H. Sutherland Award for distinguished research. He also received awards from the American Justice Institute, the Western Society of Criminology, the National Organization of Victim Assistance, and the Association of Certified Fraud Examiners (ACFE). He was president of the ACFE from 1992 to 2002 and former president of the American Society of Criminology.

Keynotes in Criminology and Criminal Justice Series

WHITE-COLLAR AND CORPORATE CRIME

[1]

ENTER "WHITE-COLLAR CRIME"

The term "white-collar crime" entered the English language on a cold, blustery winter evening in Philadelphia two days after Christmas in the year 1939, at a time in which the United States was suffering from the pangs of a severe decade-long economic depression, a period that poet W.H. Auden described as "a low dishonest decade" and philosopher Isiah Berlin called "the dark and leaden thirties."[1] Philadelphia was hosting the thirty-fourth annual meeting of the American Sociological Society, a group that, more embarrassed than amused by its acronym ASS, soon would decide that it preferred to be known as the American Sociological Association (ASA). The Philadelphia gathering, held jointly with the American Economic Association, was at the Benjamin Franklin Hotel on Ninth and Chestnut streets in the city's downtown area, where rates ran from $3.50 to $6.00 for a night's lodging. Those who attended the evening session in the hotel's Crystal Room were to hear what undoubtedly remains, some two-thirds of a century later, the most memorable presidential address in the scholarly group's history.

That day's newspapers carried an item that touched glancingly on business wrongdoing that the evening's speaker labeled "white-collar crime," coining a term that forever after would remain implanted in the consciousness of academics and the public throughout the world. Al Capone, a gangster extraordinaire, had been admitted to a Baltimore hospital with an undisclosed ailment that later was diagnosed as neurosyphilis. Capone became a footnote in the story of white-collar crime when he lamented that his behavior was no different from that of society's upper-class lawbreakers.

1

This was at a time when the sale of liquor was against the law: "They call Capone a bootlegger," he complained to a newspaper reporter. "Yes. It's bootleg while it's on the truck, but when your host hands it to you on a silver platter, it's hospitality." When Capone was convicted on a charge of income tax evasion, he asked, "Why don't they go after all these bankers who took advantage of thousands of poor people . . . . in [Depression-era] bank failures. Isn't it a lot worse to take the last few dollars some small family has saved than to sell a little beer, a little alky."[2] Capone found his way into the evening's address on white-collar crime in a reference to a phrase that he used about upper-class lawbreaking, designating it as "the legitimate rackets."[3]

The speaker on that Wednesday evening, December 27, 1939, was Edwin H. Sutherland, the American Sociological Society's twenty-ninth president. He was fifty-six years old and a professor at Indiana University. A historian of the discipline wrote almost half a century later that Sutherland was a man about whom "little doubt exists but that [he] was the most popular criminologist of all time, truly a 'pioneer' in the field."[4] The title of Sutherland's talk given in the program was "The White Collar Criminal," but on publication it had been changed to "White-Collar Criminality." The address amended and enlarged in a fundamental way the manner in which the study of crime would come to be viewed throughout the world by focusing upon a form of lawbreaking that had heretofore been almost totally ignored by criminological scholars.

Sutherland was introduced by Thomas S. Gates, the president of the University of Pennsylvania. Gates, a lawyer, had been a banker and industrialist before he began his 15-year term as head of the university. The situation was not without irony: Gates would serve as secretary of defense in President Dwight Eisenhower's cabinet twenty years later, from 1959 to 1961, and then become president and later chairman and chief executive officer of the Morgan Guaranty Trust Company. The company's founder, J. P. Morgan, was one of the richest men in the United States and his business tactics would earn him a position on the roster of commercial buccaneers who would be labeled "robber barons."[5] Gates obviously would not have been pleased when Sutherland quoted A. B. Stickney, a railroad president, as telling sixteen other railroad magnates during a meeting at Morgan's home in 1890: "I have the utmost respect for you gentlemen, individually, but as railroad presidents I wouldn't trust you with my watch out of my sight."[6] Of Morgan himself, the British writer Harold Nicholson, who knew him well, would write in his diary: "There was about him a touch of madness or something immoral and abnormal. He had the mind of a super-criminal and the character of a saint."[7]

Sutherland's talk, some 5,200 words when subsequently published, began with the observation that the economists in the audience, while well acquainted with the methods of business, rarely looked at these methods in terms of crime, while sociologists, though often students of criminal behavior, rarely considered it as an ingredient of business. Sutherland proclaimed that what he was about to lay out represented an attempt to integrate the economic and sociological views; it was "a comparison of crime in the upper or white-collar class, composed of respectable or at least respected business and professional men, and crime in the lower class, composed of persons of low socioeconomic status."[8] This was Sutherland's initial effort to indicate what he intended to include in the embrace of white-collar crime, foreshadowing what would become an unending obsession in white-collar crime scholarship to determine a proper definition of the subject.

Definitional difficulties and dilemmas aside, Sutherland's indictment was all-embracing: "White-collar criminality is found in every occupation, as can be discovered readily in casual conversation with a representative of an occupation by asking him, 'What crooked practices are found in your occupation?'"[9]

The most important crime news, Sutherland claimed, was more likely to be found on the financial pages of newspapers than on the front pages. This point was echoed two decades later by Alan Dershowitz, then a senior at Yale Law School, when he looked at the coverage of the General Electric antitrust crimes.[10] It is significant, however, that when the Enron accounting scandals erupted, Howell Raines, then the managing editor of the *New York Times*, insisted that the paper display the stories of corporate corruption prominently and continuously on its first page.[11]

To buttress his position, Sutherland rattled off a roster of misdeeds by physicians, whom he presumed were probably more honest than most professionals. The list included abortions (illegal at the time), sale of prohibited narcotics, services to underworld kingpins, such as cosmetic surgery to help them avoid recognition and capture, fraudulent reports in accident cases, unnecessary treatment, fake specialists, and fee splitting. Fee splitting, unlawful in most states, involves doctors referring patients to a surgeon who will provide them with the largest kickback rather than one they believe will do the best work. Most of these medical misdeeds and many others occur today—perhaps in even greater numbers than in Sutherland's time.[12] In the business world, Sutherland saw flagrant double-dealing and he deplored the fact that the loyalties of regulatory officials charged with discovering and prosecuting business crime often lay with the criminals. For Sutherland the situation was no different than having a football coach refereeing a game in which his own team was playing.

Sutherland's indictments and accusations kept coming in a cascade. He pointed out that before the Securities and Exchange Commission had been formed in 1933, an accountant estimated that 80 percent of the financial declarations of corporations were misleading, a figure that may be lower today, but, as recent notorious corporate scandals indicate, remains far from insignificant. Sutherland relied on an insider, James M. Beck, at one time Solicitor General of the United States, to sum up his case: "Diogenes would have been hard put to it to find a honest man in the Wall Street I knew as a corporation lawyer," Beck maintained.[13]

Sutherland took the position that politics, however rotten, was a less tainted enterprise than business. For this judgment he relied on writers who presumably were in a position to know, including John T. Flynn, a highly regarded investigative reporter and the former chief researcher for the US Senate committee that had produced a seething indictment of American arms manufacturers before World War I. While the report granted that the companies were not the sole cause of the war and the immense casualties suffered on both sides, it found that they had behaved in ways that were "against the peace of the world" and that they were "self-interested organizations" that had "frightened nations into military activity." An agent for the Colt arms manufacturer told the committee that selling arms abroad had "brought into play the most despicable side of human nature, lies, deceit, hypocrisy, greed, and graft occupying a most prominent part in the transactions." The committee scornfully noted the response of the businesses to proposed restrictions on the sale of weapons overseas:

> Munitions companies provided active opposition to proposals for arms limitations and showed resentment toward them, contempt for those responsible for them, and violation of such controls whenever established, and of rich profiting whenever such proposals failed.[14]

Flynn was quoted by Sutherland as maintaining that "[t]he average politician is the merest amateur in the gentle art of graft, compared with his brother in business."[15] To this was added the comment by Walter Lippmann, a particularly highly regarded political commentator: "Poor as they are, the standards of public life are so much more social than those of business that financiers who enter politics regard themselves as philanthropists."[16]

According to Sutherland, political graft almost always involves collusion between politicians and businessmen, but prosecutions are generally limited to the politicians. Judge [Martin T.] Manton was found guilty of accepting $664,000 in bribes,[17] but the six or eight important commercial concerns that paid the bribes have not been prosecuted. [Tom] Pendergast, the late boss of Kansas City, was convicted for failure to report as part of his income $315,000 received in bribes from insurance companies, but the insurance companies that paid the bribes have not been prosecuted.[18] In an investigation of embezzlement by the president of a bank, at least a dozen other violations of law that were related to this embezzlement and involved most of the other officers of the bank and the officers of the cleaning house, were discovered, but none of the others were prosecuted.[19]

The accuracy of this observation, both in Sutherland's time and now, remains uncertain, though case studies appear to support the position that those who take bribes are treated more severely than those who offer them. For one thing, we have no sure sense of the extent and nature of bribery. As an in-depth study of the practice has observed, "[h]istorically, prosecutors have depended on chance to bring cases to their attention,"[20] and it is not unlikely that chance will turn up violations of a certain nature rather than an acceptable sample of instances of bribery.

A recent case involving Congressman James A. Trafficant, Jr., illustrates Sutherland's theme. Trafficant did favors for corporate executives who showed their appreciation by providing equipment for his farm, money, a boat, and similar tokens of gratitude. Trafficant, an Ohio Democrat, became only the second member of Congress to be expelled since the Civil War. The first was involved in the Abscam sting operation run by the FBI in 1980.[21] Other bribe suspects had resigned when it became apparent that their legislating days were numbered or, if election time was near, they either did not run or were defeated at the polls.

Trafficant differed in the doggedness and brazenness with which he fought the allegations. Bluster (not without an edge of biting humor) characterized his response to the hearings of the House Committee on Standards of Official Conduct.[22] Most of its members, he told the press, were so dumb that they could throw themselves at the ground and miss. The House voted 420 to 1 to expel Trafficant: the lone negative vote came from Gary Condit, a California representative, defeated in the subsequent election, who was under fire for an affair with an intern and his possible implication in her disappearance and murder.

The failure to punish the bribers in this case and numerous others supports Sutherland's theme. The reason may lie in the different conditions that prevail in regard to government officials and politicians who are bribe takers. For one thing, there probably is general agreement among onlookers that it is more malevolent to solicit, demand, or accept a bribe than to offer one. For another, enforcement agents and prosecutors are themselves part of the government, and they understand it better than they understand the ethos of business and therefore are better able to deal with offenders who operate in the same realm they inhabit. Also, the paper trail, so crucial in white-collar prosecutions, is very likely to be more accessible in the political arena than in the business world. In addition, there generally is greater publicity to be obtained by going after a government official, particularly a prominent one, than proceeding against a less publicly visible corporate figure.

Whatever the common fate of those who take bribes, white-collar criminals in general, Sutherland believed, are likely to be ignored or treated in ways other than by being prosecuted criminally. He pointed out that they do not regard themselves and are not seen as criminals by the general public or by criminologists. To make the point that prosecutions were aimed at small fish, while the sharks and whales went unmolested, Sutherland quoted Daniel Drew, a railroad speculator: "Law is like a cobweb; it's made for flies and the smaller kind of insects, so to speak, but lets the big bumblebees break through. When technicalities of the law stood in my way, I have always been able to brush them aside easy as anything"[23] As a onetime teacher of Greek, Sutherland perhaps should have known that Drew had stolen this maxim, as he stole so much else, from an earlier—some 2,500 years earlier—source. In 1166, John of Salisbury, exiled in France during the conflict between the

English king and the Archbishop of Canterbury, conveyed his cynicism in a letter to an English bishop: "Civil laws," he wrote, "as Anacharsis the Scythian said, are like spiders' webs, catching flies and letting greater flying things through."[24] Anacharsis had made his statement in the late sixth or early fifth century before the Christian era, and it was widely circulated by the Roman writer Valerius Maximus,[25] among several others.[26] In 1709, the satirist Jonathan Swift, author of *Gulliver's Travels*, also cribbed the epigram, noting in *An Essay upon the Faculties of the Mind* that "laws are like cobwebs, which may catch small flies, but let wasps and hornets break through."[27] Later, John Adams, the second president of the United States, explicitly adapted Anacharsis' axiom to the ancient Greek constitution, which he declared "was but a cobweb, to bind the poor, while the rich would easily break through it."[28]

Sutherland also included in his address an observation that has been echoed through the years by virtually every person who addresses issues of white-collar crime: "The financial cost of white-collar crime is probably several times as great as the financial cost of all the crimes which are customarily included in the 'crime problem.'"[29] He ridiculed theories of crime that blamed factors such as poverty, broken homes, and Freudian fixations for illegal behavior, noting that a healthy upbringing and an intact psyche had not deterred monstrous amounts of lawbreaking by persons in positions of power. In a memorable paragraph, Sutherland later expressed both this view and his lifelong distaste for psychiatric theorizing:

> We have no reason to think that General Motors has an inferiority complex or that the Aluminum Company of America has a frustration-aggression complex or that U.S. Steel has an Oedipus complex, or that the Armour company has a death wish or that the Duponts desire to return to the womb. The assumption that an offender must have some such pathological distortion of the intellect or the emotions seems to me absurd, and if it is absurd regarding the crimes of businessmen, it is equally absurd regarding the crimes of persons in the lower economic class.[30]

This psychiatric antipathy also was on display in a later article in which Sutherland insisted that "there is no more reason for turning over to the psychiatrist the complete supervision of a criminal found to be psychopathic than turning over to the dentist the complete supervision of a criminal who is found to have dental cavities."[31] Sutherland undoubtedly would have agreed with the critical observation of Thomas Szasz, himself a psychiatrist, that "psychiatry—in contrast to the nonmedical branches of social science—has acquired much social prestige and power through an essentially misleading association with medicine."[32]

The standard explanatory menu of sociology fared no better at Sutherland's hands. The idea that criminal behavior in general is due to poverty or to the psychopathic or sociopathic conditions associated with poverty could now be shown to be invalid, Sutherland maintained. That kind of simplistic thinking, he said, was wrong because it was based on a biased sample of law-breakers that ignored white-collar criminals, and it did so because criminologists, "for reasons of convenience and ignorance rather than of principle," have restricted their research largely to criminal and juvenile court cases.[33] Sutherland maintained that such work supported the errone-ous cliché that the criminal of today was the problem child of yesterday, and he insisted that the belief that the causes of criminality are to be located almost exclusively in childhood was a fallacious view. In this regard, he pre-sciently challenged the self-control theory of Michael Gottfredson and Travis Hirschi, which would come to dominate the realm of criminological theory some sixty years later; its progenitors would claim that its tenets em-braced white-collar as well as all other forms of crime as well as some analo-gous acts.[34] Sutherland's own explanation for both white-collar and lower-class crime was a set of postulates that he labeled "differential asso-ciation." He outlined it in the following terms:

> The hypothesis which is here suggested as a substitute for the conventional theories is that white-collar criminality, just as other systematic criminality, is learned; that it is learned in direct or indirect association with those who already practice the behavior; and that those who learn this criminal behavior are segregated from frequent and intimate contacts with law-abiding behavior. Whether a person becomes a criminal or not is deter-mined largely by the comparative frequency and intimacy of his contacts with the two types of behavior. This may be called the principle of differential association. . . . Those who become white-collar criminals generally start their careers in good

neighborhoods and good homes, graduate from colleges with some idealism, and with little selection on their part, get into particular business situations in which criminality is practically a folkway and are inducted into that system of behavior just as into any other folkway.[35]

Social disorganization also was said to contribute to white-collar crime because people in the United States were not solidly antagonistic to such behavior. The law was pressing in one direction, Sutherland maintained, while other forces were pressing in the opposite direction: the rules for how the game should be played in business were in conflict with legal requirements, and individuals typically were more concerned with their immediate self-interest than with social welfare in general.

We will examine Sutherland's interpretative ideas in a later chapter when we take up the matter of definitions and theoretical explanations of white-collar crime. Let it only be said here that his theory has proven to be no sounder than the competing causal interpretations that he attacked.

The process by which the term "white-collar crime" came to be implanted in Sutherland's thinking is not altogether clear. In a 1932 article he maintained that newcomers to America are exposed to a culture that features "exaggeration, misrepresentation, sharp practices, graft, grasping competition, and disregard of human beings" and that they are "isolated from the private culture of America as represented in the homes and neighborhoods of the older American communities." But he granted that this position, while it might go a short way toward explaining immigrant lawbreaking, "certainly does not explain the financial crimes of the white-collar classes."[36] Two years later, categorizing the backgrounds of unemployed men living in Chicago shelters during the nationwide economic depression, Sutherland classified "professional men, business men, clerks, salesmen, accountants, and men who previously held minor political positions" as "white collar workers."[37]

Sutherland's first linkage of "white-collar" and "crime" occurred in the 1934 edition of his textbook when he stated that the political and economic landscape in the United States was undergoing rapid change, but that legal codes were not keeping pace. This gap, Sutherland wrote, encouraged the emergence of a new type of law violator, the "white-collar criminaloid." "These white-collar criminaloids," Sutherland claimed, "are by far the most dangerous to society of any type of criminals from the point of view of effects on private property and social institutions."[38]

"Criminaloid" was a term that had been coined several decades earlier by sociologist Edward A. Ross in a rousing article for the prestigious *Atlantic Monthly* in which he castigated "those who prosper by flagitious practices which have not yet come under the effective ban of public opinion." Criminaloids, Ross fumed, "reveal in their faces nothing of the wolf or vulture. Nature has not foredoomed them to evil by a double dose of lust, cruelty, malice, greed, or jealousy. They are not degenerates tormented by monstrous cravings. They want nothing more than all of us want—money, power, consideration—in a word, success; but they are in a hurry and they are not particular about the means." In addition, Ross noted:

> The criminaloid counterfeits the good citizen. He takes care to meet all the conventional tests—flag worship, old-soldier sentiment, observance of all the national holidays, perfervid patriotism, party regularity and support. Full well he knows that giving a fountain or a park or establishing a college chair on the Neolithic drama or the elegiac poetry of the Chaldeans will more than outweigh the dodging of taxes, the grabbing of streets, and the corrupting of city councils.[39]

Ross echoed the sentiments of most of the early founders of sociology who saw their mission as employing social science to improve human life. "I wouldn't give a snap of my finger for the pussyfooting sociologist," Ross wrote in his autobiography.[40]

Sutherland's familiarity with Ross's work is shown in a letter he wrote in 1916 noting that "last night, I talked to a county Sunday School convention, along the lines of Ross' idea of modern sin."[41] Ross's wrath at the behavior of those he identified as criminaloids, a group that included the exceedingly wealthy railroad robber baron Leland Stanford, played a part in his forced departure from Stanford University on the initiative of Stanford's widow, the school's cofounder of the University. She had become "weary" of Professor Ross and told the University president that he should be dismissed because of his "dangerous socialism." "Because of his ability and because of his brightness," Jane Lathrop Stanford noted, "he is a desirable factor to the socialistic element" and "he must go." Ross went—and became a fixture thereafter at the University of Wisconsin.[42] Ross's firing has always hovered as a cautionary lesson to scholars who take on a vengeful establishment. In times when scapegoats for political uneasiness were required, most notably in the witch-hunting period of Senator Joseph McCarthy, research and writing on white-collar crime tends to go out of favor. To pursue the subject was seen as a threat to one's career.

Daniel Drew, the railroad speculator quoted earlier, is a perfect illustration of Ross's observation. It would be difficult to locate a businessman more viciously unscrupulous than Drew. "Business slobbers a fellow up," Drew wrote. "It's like teaching a calf to drink out of a pai—you're sure to get splashed and dirty. Business is a scramble for cash."[43] Rather than a chair in Neolithic drama, Drew used part of his ill-gotten loot to found the Drew Theological Seminary, now renamed Drew University, located in Madison, New Jersey.

In Sutherland's day, metropolitan newspapers routinely took heed of the proceedings of national scholarly organizations such as the American Sociological Society. Indeed, academics in those days tended to be much closer to the seats of power than they are today. Ross, for instance, was a regular correspondent of President Theodore Roosevelt.[44] Today, on the rare occasions when the media deign to cover gatherings such as those of social scientists and humanists, they are likely to treat them as tribal gatherings and to poke fun at the jargon and what their reporters, themselves much better educated than in earlier days, are likely to regard as ideological posturing. Reporters also work the hallways and the lobbies at today's scholarly meetings and with some justification are likely to compare them to slave markets, where somewhat frantic job candidates exchange woeful tales of their efforts to get a foot into tenure-track academic doors.

Things were different in 1939. The *Philadelphia Public Ledger* prominently displayed a news report about Sutherland's address. The headline read: "Poverty Belittled as Crime Factor." Given the tyranny of headline space boundaries, the writer had selected but one causal factor that had been debunked by Sutherland: there also was feeble-mindedness, psychopathic deviations, and slums. The reporter had no difficulty interpreting the tone of Sutherland's remarks, labeling his talk a "withering denunciation" of white-collar criminality. Sutherland was said to have presented a "revolutionary approach to the study of criminal behavior" to an "astonished audience" and to have "figuratively heaved scores of sociological textbooks into a waste basket."[45]

The *New York Times*, with a story on its first page, offered a more sedate report on Sutherland's address but featured it on its front page. The headline read "Hits Criminality in White Collars," and there were three subheads. "Dr. Sutherland Says the Cost of Duplicity in High Places Exceeds Burglary Losses," while below that, in capital letters, was: "'Robber Barons' Outdone." The final subhead attended to a paper that had been presented by William Healy, a psychiatrist and director of the Judge Baker Guidance Center in Boston. It read: "Plan to Put Youthful Offenders Under New State Law."

The *Times* reporter also called attention to the aggressive intensity of Sutherland's presentation, noting the "sharp attack" on white-collar crime. Deep into his story, the reporter, as had his Philadelphia counterpart, reproduced a point made by Sutherland that was largely overlooked until much later when, as we shall see, Susan Shapiro in a revisionist effort attempted to build a theoretical framework around the idea. The seventh paragraph of the *Times* story read:

> The speaker said that white-collar crime in business and
> the professions consisted chiefly in "violations of delegated
> or implied trust" and might be reduced to the categories,
> "misrepresentation of asset values and duplicity in the
> manipulation of money."[46]

Both major newspapers plucked from the speech the sound-byte phrase that white-collar crime was much like "taking candy from a baby," and both harked to Sutherland's point that more crime news appeared in their financial sections than on their front pages.

Sutherland's presidential address was unusually hard hitting, considering that his audience of academics at the time was strongly committed to what then was valued as "scientific neutrality."[47] Later, social scientists came to recognize that virtually any inquiry, most notably in the selection of the topic, carries an inherent value judgment, and some spelled out the personal views they had brought to their research endeavor and detailed what they believed were the policy implications of their inquiries. A psychiatrist, Robert J. Lifton, discussed such later stands particularly well. He advocated what he called a combination of "advocacy and detachment" that would involve "articulating one's inevitable moral advocacies, rather than bootlegging them in via a claim to absolute moral neutrality; and, at the same time, maintaining a sufficient detachment to apply the technical and scientific principles of one's discipline."[48] Equally apt is Janet Malcolm's conclusion about the posture of scientific neutrality:

> Writing cannot be done in a state of desirelessness. The pose of fair-mindedness, the charade of evenhandedness, the theoretical ruses; if they were genuine, if the writer *actually* didn't care one way or the other how things came out, he would not bestir himself to represent them.[49]

Probably the most disingenuous words in Sutherland's presidential address were uttered in the very first moments that he spoke. He claimed that his talk was for "the purpose of developing the theories of criminal behavior, not for the purpose of muckraking or for reforming anything but criminology."[50] This was disingenuous. Sutherland was on the warpath; nobody hearing his speech or reading his subsequent book could sensibly conclude otherwise.

It was ten years after his presidential address that Sutherland published his classic monograph *White Collar Crime*. He was a particularly slow worker when it came to scholarship: he was wont to spend his evenings in card playing, a recreation forbidden (along with dancing, smoking, and drinking alcoholic beverages) in the strict Baptist home he had grown up in. Administrative work also took a good deal of his time and energy. Sutherland also suffered from stomach ulcers.

White Collar Crime shows signs of having been written in some haste. I once asked Donald Cressey, who had been a graduate student with Sutherland and who was responsible for the later editions of Sutherland's classic criminology text, if Sutherland might have been having health problems—he died a year after *White Collar Crime* was published. Cressey thought not. "Sutherland's father lived until he was 95," Cressey said, "and Sutherland thought he'd live forever."

A glaring omission in *White Collar Crime* is the identity of the specific corporations who had violated the law and thereby drawn Sutherland's attention. They are designated only by letters and numbers. Sutherland, seemingly somewhat uneasy about this tactic, offers two explanations: first, that the identity of street criminals is often concealed in scientific writings and, second, that "the objective of the book, which is the theory of criminal behavior, can be better attained without directing attention in an invidious manner to the behavior of particular corporations."[51] The real story is that Dryden Press, the book's publisher, was nervous about possible lawsuits and requested that corporate identities be excised. They pointed out that Sutherland had called a number of corporations "criminals" though they had not been so adjudicated in a criminal court. If Dryden were to be sued, its assets would be frozen to cover a possible unfavorable verdict and its operations would have to be severely curtailed. Besides, Indiana University was the recipient of considerable largess from Eli Lilly, a major pharmaceutical company, and Sutherland was concerned that the company might be offended by so frontal an attack on the corporate world. Sutherland eliminated the corporate names as well as a chapter titled "Three Case Histories" that contained detailed accounts of episodes of wrongdoing by the American Smelting and Refining Company, the US Rubber Company, and the Pittsburgh Coal Company. It was not until 1983 that an unexpurgated edition of the book, the manuscript of which had been in the possession of Karl Schuessler, a colleague of Sutherland, was published by Yale University Press.[52]

White Collar Crime is as inflammatory as the presidential address, with bursts of exasperation, vituperation, and indignation. The following is but one illustration:

> ... the utility corporations for two generations or more
> have engaged in organized propaganda to develop
> favorable sentiments. They devoted much attention to the
> public schools in an effort to mold the opinion of children.[53]
> Perhaps no group except the Nazis have paid so much
> attention to indoctrinating the youth of the land with ideas
> favorable to a special interest, and it is doubtful whether
> even the Nazis were less bound by considerations of honesty
> in their propaganda.[54]

Such vituperation seems surprising from a person who uniformly was described by those who knew him as "imbued with sincerity and objectivity," "soft spoken," "a man of paternal wisdom," who "never taught in terms of sarcasm, ridicule or abuse."[55] Jerome Hall, a colleague at Indiana University, observed that Sutherland was distinguished by "an attitude of extraordinary objectivity and thorough inquiry maintained on a high level" and was a man who "knows how to keep his feelings and personality from intruding into the discussion."[56]

The subject of white-collar crime clearly impinged on a raw nerve in Sutherland's psyche, driving him to depart from the demeanor that colleagues found so amiably admirable and intellectually dignified. An indication of how aroused Sutherland could become at what he viewed as white-collar offenses and offenders appears in a letter he wrote in 1942, when the United States was engaged in World War II, to the secretary-manager of the Hoosier Motor Club in Indianapolis, a man who had urged the state's residents to petition their congressional representatives to vote to postpone national gas rationing that was designed to see that adequate supplies would be available to overseas troops. Sutherland found the secretary-manager's proposal "absurd," writing to him that those who favored it "had a financial interest in promoting the driving of automobiles," and that they were "placing personal interest ahead of the national interest." Thoroughly infuriated, Sutherland concluded:

> This is an effort to interfere with the successful prosecution of the war and is subversive. I feel that the government is entirely justified in sending the F.B.I. to investigate you. They may find that your action is directed from Berlin, or they may find that it is merely selfish interest in your own welfare; the effects are the same.[57]

Sutherland wrote the letter as a private citizen; he did not use university stationery and gave his home address. The recipient replied with a batch of literature and the observation that Sutherland owed him an apology for "probably the most insulting . . . letter I have ever received."[58]

Sutherland immediately retracted his personal attack, though he did so in a letter which launched a further assault on the motives of the Hoosier Motor Club. "I apologize for the personal reference in my former letter,"

Sutherland now wrote. "My letter was written in anger against your movement but I know nothing whatever about you as a person and had no justification in making personal statements about you." But he would "retract
nothing . . . regarding the organized effort to delay the rationing program,"
and insisted that when rationing came, as it most surely would, "all the
literature you are distributing will encourage the blackmarkets and crook-
edness which you so freely predict."[59]

In *White Collar Crime* Sutherland examined a roster of corporate offenses, including antitrust violations, false advertising, theft of trade se-
crets, and bribery, concluding that the "rap sheets" of big businesses
resembled those of professional predators, such as con men, burglars, and
bank robbers. He maintained that the failure to attend satisfactorily to
crimes of the powerful was a result of the relationship between white-
collar offenders and those who determine what will be regarded as serious
wrongdoing. Newspapers, for instance, themselves skirting the spirit of
the child labor laws by employing minors as delivery boys and girls and
labeling them "independent contractors," hesitated to highlight violations of regulatory laws by other business enterprises lest their own tactics might come under scrutiny. The papers also depended upon advertiser
goodwill, and many were reluctant to bite the hand that fed them.

The legal inequities noted by Sutherland that surround white-collar
crime and criminals were discussed by a later writer who derided the
concept of fair and impartial justice:

> Saying that all are equal before the law . . . simply means that
> poor people and wealthy people will be treated exactly *as they
> are*: the poor as poor and the wealthy as wealthy. Since the law
> refuses to recognize the built-in inequality between poor and
> wealthy, thereby giving extra consideration to the poor so that
> genuine equality may be achieved, no real justice is ever attained
> through this method of equality.[60]

This is a situation crucial to an understanding of the manner in which
white-collar crimes are legislated and dealt with. "'Equality before law' is
a high-sounding phrase," the historian Margaret James wrote, "which
conceals great actual inequality, putting the poor and ignorant at a disadvantage as compared with the rich and well informed and resulting in

more practical abuses than a system of arbitrary decrees."[61] Best known is the aphorism of the novelist Anatole France, who wrote of the "majestic equality of the law that forbids the rich as well as the poor to sleep under bridges, to beg in the streets and to steal bread."[62] There are others as well who have contributed to this chorus. The English playwright and essayist George Bernard Shaw wrote that "while a poor person snatches a loaf of bread from a baker's counter and is promptly run into jail," the businessman "snatches bread from the tables of hundreds of widows and orphans and simple credulous souls who do not know the ways of company promoters; and, as likely as not, he is run into Parliament."[63]

Sutherland emphasized that judges, who themselves often are the beneficiaries of political processes that are less than wholesome, are likely to take an indulgent attitude toward law breaking by business people and professionals who had attended the same colleges as the judges, belonged to the same churches, and lived in the same upscale neighborhoods. In this regard, a Washington, DC judge observed in court that he would "not penalize a businessman trying to make a living when there are felons out on the street."[64] In addition, jurors are bound to be impressed by articulate and well-dressed corporate executives and by the well-paid and extremely skilled attorneys who defend them in those rare instances when their offenses lead to a criminal trial.

A later attempt to test the gist of Sutherland's position scrutinized the opinions of liberal and conservative judges on the US Supreme Court, finding that the conservative judges were more sympathetic to the claims of white-collar offenders than to those of street criminals. The reverse was true for the liberal jurists. When the judges were confronted with white-collar crime cases, the researchers found that they seemed to lose the philosophical bearings that marked their other decisions and that the rhetoric in their rulings on such cases was "both hypocritical and result-driven," the last phrase meaning that the justices appeared to start with a conclusion and then to hunt for more or less acceptable reasons to support the predetermined stance.[65]

But the evidence is far from one-sided. Recent appellate rulings appear to reflect the premise that possession of the attributes of a successful life is not a sufficient reason for leniency but rather aggravates the wrongdoing. In a 1994 case involving a corporate figure accused of conspiring to sell adulterated orange juice, a judge, obviously unimpressed, noted that "it is usual and ordinary, in the prosecution of white-collar offenses involving high-ranking corporate officials . . . , to find that a defendant was involved as a leader in community charities, civil organizations, and church efforts."[66] Carrying that logic further, a judge in a later case in which a hospital manager was convicted of paying bribes to doctors to route patients to his facility noted, while rejecting an appeal for a reduced sentence, that "[e]xcellent character references are not out of the ordinary for an executive who commits a white-collar crime; one would be surprised to see a person rise to an elevated position in business if people did not think highly of him or her."[67]

Nonetheless, the impact of the status of a white-collar offender was evident when federal investigators sought evidence against Spiro Agnew, then the vice president of the United States, for accepting bribes. They adopted the policy of calling persons under investigation in that case "bad men" in order to condition themselves to their task. "It was one thing to dispose of a mugger," they reasoned, "but quite another thing when it came to men very much like themselves—college-educated, middle class, articulate. These were not street people, but men with roots in the community. The humiliation of jail was total and absolute."[68]

Sutherland insisted that the white-collar offenses he studied were truly criminal acts, however the legal system might respond to them. His position provoked strong criticism from sociologists with legal training, who argued that Sutherland was slapping a "criminal" label on persons who had been dealt with civilly or administratively.[69] Sutherland's defense relied on an analogy to medicine: no matter what treatment that a patient receives—be it the poultices and bloodletting of earlier times or streptomycin in Sutherland's day—a person who has tuberculosis is still a tubercular person. He insisted that someone who commits a white-collar crime remains a criminal if the offense is undiscovered, or ignored, or if the person is sentenced to prison for it. He would seem to have the better in this dispute, although he would have to admit that he was substituting his own judgment for that of the formal process of criminal adjudication. In doing so, he could introduce personal biases into the manner in which he determined whether or not a white-collar individual truly deserved to be considered a "criminal." Sutherland would argue that similar kinds of bias distort the way the justice system responds to acts that reasonably should be regarded as crimes.

The debate between Sutherland and some lawyers did not end with the disputes that arose at the time he was writing. Jerome Hall, a personal friend and a colleague teaching at the Indiana University Law School, repeated the jurisprudential reservations about white-collar crime but also observed that the foray of Sutherland and some of his followers into the subject provided "factual data that are essential in future studies deemed to advance criminology and, equally, to solve some very difficult legal problems."[70]

Sutherland regarded white-collar crime as generally more consequential than the run-of-the-mill street offenses, insisting that white-collar lawbreaking was more likely than street offenses to tear at the heart of a social system and to render its citizens cynical and selfish:

> White collar crimes violate trust and therefore create distrust; this lowers social morale and produces social disorganization. Many of the white collar crimes attack the fundamental principles of the American institutions. Ordinary crimes, on the other hand, produce little effect on social institutions or social organization.[71]

The term "white-collar criminal" found its way into *The Oxford English Dictionary*, where it was defined as "applied to a person who takes advantages of the special knowledge or responsibility of his position to commit a non-violent, often financial crime."[72] The "nonviolent" element in the definition is arguable. Environmental pollution, failure to meet the requirements for coal mine safety, and medical malpractice all can have lethal consequences and all are regarded as white-collar crimes. This point is well conveyed by sociologist Lonnie Athens, who has conducted research on homicide. Athens discusses a particularly brutal assault by a man on a woman, a stranger to him, who had insulted him when she saw him peering into her unoccupied camper. Criminals who commit such heinous crimes, Athens observes, "are the most dangerous violent criminals in our society." Then he adds: "With perhaps the exception of certain white-collar criminals whose actions jeopardize the health or safety of large numbers of people."[73]

Sutherland's monograph contains a curious final section in which he presents case histories of petty shenanigans of people such as shoe salesmen. These vignettes were largely collected from students, and they add to the confusion about precisely what it was that Sutherland meant by the term "white-collar crime." The gap between business people in positions of power and the stories Sutherland offers is glaring—and puzzling. Here is one example:

> A man came in and asked if we had any high, tan button shoes. I told him that we had no shoes of that style. He thanked me and walked out. . . . The floor-walker asked me what the man wanted. I told him what the man asked for and what I replied. The floor-walker said angrily: "Damn it! We're not here to sell what they want. We're here to sell what we've got." He went on to instruct that when a customer came into the store, the first thing to do was to get him to sit down and take off his shoe so that he couldn't get out of the store. "If we don't have what he wants," he said, "bring him something else and try to interest him in that style. If he's still uninterested, inform the floor-walker and he will send one of the regular salesmen, and if that doesn't work, a third salesman will be sent to him. Our policy is that no customer gets out of the store without a sale until at least three salesmen have worked on him. By that time, he feels that he must be a crank and will usually buy something whether he wants to or not."[74]

The neophyte shoe seller learned that shoe sizes were marked in code so that the customer could not decipher them, and that it was usual to bring the nearest size available if the one that would fit best was not in stock, and to lie to the customer if he or she asked about the actual size of the offered shoes. The rule was to sell everyone a pair of shoes, preferably a pair that fit but some other pair if necessary. Clerks received a bonus for selling out-of-style shoes, called "spiffs." The trick was to fob them off on gullible customers by telling them it was the latest style or that it was an older style that now was coming back in favor.

White Collar Crime was heralded with widespread praise and a few reservations. Hermann Mannheim of the London School of Economics stated that it was a "milestone" and he praised Sutherland's "ingenuity, persistence, and courage in exposing [white-collar crime's] meaning, extent, and danger to society." He thought that the book "should become the starting point of a new line of research.[75] Selden Bacon of Rutgers University, better known for his research on alcoholism than any work on crime, thought that Sutherland's book was "restricted and unbalanced," but nonetheless called it "daring" because it "challenged the arbiters of the alleged science of criminology."[76] The "alleged" in the review represented a gratuitous slap at current studies of crime and was obviously based on a recent unremittingly critical review of the field by Jerome Michael, a law professor, and Mortimer J. Adler, a philosopher,[77] whose attack on criminological knowledge had persuaded Sutherland to do some fine tuning on his own efforts to encase his findings in a theoretical framework.

Writing in the *Harvard Law Review*, Robert Sorenson noted that Sutherland had presented "a deadly exposé of a way of life which society complacently accepts." He called Sutherland's emphases "realistic" and "deserving of excited promotion rather than mere reviewing."[78] In an extensive analysis of the book in the *Yale Law Review*, Thomas I. Emerson noted a number of errors that undoubtedly arose from Sutherland's unfamiliarity with aspects of jurisprudence. Emerson hoped that "many others will explore the path that [Sutherland] has opened."[79]

There are some clues along the way regarding the route by which Sutherland developed his ideas and attitudes about white-collar crime. His great-grandparents had migrated to Canada from Scotland and settled in St. John's in the province of New Brunswick.[80] George Sutherland, Edwin's father, was born there in 1840. Depressed economic conditions drove the family to migrate to a farm on the outskirts of Eau Claire, Wisconsin. Sutherland's father earned a divinity degree at the "old" University of Chicago, which had been founded by Baptists in 1857, and was closed thirty years later due to a lack of funds. After graduation, he took a job teaching at the Nebraska Baptist Seminary in Gibbon, where Edwin, the third of seven children, was born on August 13, 1883. "Some seem to think it was too large a number for respectable people to have," Sutherland's father would say of his brood. "On the meager salary I received, we found it hard to feed and clothe them. But when they had grown up, when at times they gathered together in the old homestead, it looked as though there were none too many, that without them, the world would have been much poorer."[81]

Less than a year after Edwin Sutherland's birth, the family relocated in Kansas and George Sutherland served for nine years as the head of the Ottawa College history department. In 1893, the Nebraska Baptist Seminary moved to Grand Island, a city with a population of about 6,000 persons that had been founded in the quixotic belief that it would be designated the country's capital since it then was the very geographic center of the United States. The Seminary was renamed Grand Island College and George Sutherland was appointed its president.

Sutherland received his bachelor's degree in 1904 from Grand Island College. He played offensive fullback on the 1902 state championship football team; there is a picture of him in the yearbook in uniform, looking suitably fierce and formidable. He tied for a Rhodes scholarship to attend Oxford University in England, but the honor ultimately went to his competitor. Sutherland took a teaching position at Sioux Falls College in South Dakota, a Baptist institution, where he was responsible for classes in Greek, Latin, and shorthand. After he received his Ph.D. at the University of Chicago, he taught sociology at William Jewell College in Liberty, Missouri, from 1913 to 1919. The College itself provided a footnote to the history of criminal behavior: the first ride-by shooting victim of the Jessie James gang was a William Jewell student.[82] Given the publish-or-perish academic tradition of the present time, it is noteworthy that Sutherland wrote only one article in his six years at William Jewell, a piece titled "What Health Surveys Have Revealed," which appeared in the *Monthly Bulletin of the State Board of Charities and Corrections.* The college first admitted female students in 1914, when it merged with a local women's college. In the 1914–1915 yearbook, the women thanked Dr. Southerland [sic] for his acceptance of them and for his helpfulness.[83]

Personal connections with University of Chicago sociology faculty members and the department's former graduate students helped move Sutherland upward to teaching posts at the University of Illinois (1919–1926), the University of Minnesota (1926–1929), and then a period at the Bureau of Social Hygiene in New York City (1929–1930). After that, he took a research position at the University of Chicago (1931–1935) that he left for reasons that have never been clarified and took a job as the founding head of the sociology department at Indiana University. He held that position until his death while walking to his office on the morning of October 11, 1950. He was then sixty-three years old.

Sutherland undoubtedly absorbed in his youth the doctrines of the populist movement that enjoyed particularly strong support in Nebraska, the home state of William Jennings Bryan, the three-time candidate (and loser) in races for the presidency.[84] Ignatius Donnelly in his successful 1893 Populist party campaign for a seat in Congress declared that "should all other measures fail, [I favor] the enactment of laws to confiscate the real and personal property of all [business] trusts and combinations, to deny them access to the courts to enforce their claims and to withdraw from their property the protection of the law."[85] The Populist newspaper in Nebraska, the *Alliance-Independent*, in 1892 stated what it regarded as the two paramount issues facing the nation:

1. Shall the corporations, which have so long dominated and corrupted our politics. and robbed our people through extortionist charges, be retired from power, and the people given freight rates no higher than those now in force in Iowa?
2. Shall our state offices be administered by selfish men who ignore the law, and violate their official oaths that they may enrich themselves at the expense of the taxpayers, and under whose past domination the most monstrous and shameful corruption has prevailed, or shall these offices be administered by honest men in the interest of the people?[86]

Populists accepted both industrialism and capitalism, but they rejected corporate power that they believed was leading to the economic, social, and political dominance of business in America. The consolidation of wealth, in their view, constituted a menace to the continued existence of a social order in which the democratic control of industry would be possible. They sought a moral basis for capitalism—a capitalism that was humanly fulfilling—and a government that would not be devoted to business priorities but to the public interest.[87] While adherents varied in their views on specific issues, they shared a similar critique of American business practices:

> All agreed that the problems accompanying industrialization and urbanization were less technical than moral. . . . They looked

forward neither to a jungle society, based on
struggling individuals, which they saw rising about them, nor to a
pluralistic society in which the clash of interests determined the
public good. Instead, they wanted a more cooperative, less competitive society, in which the standards of behavior
informing private life informed public life as well and in which the
self-indulgent impulses of individuals were restrained.[88]

Ruth Kornhauser, an astute analyst of criminological theorizing, is one
of the few who have clearly identified the populist elements in Sutherland's
writings, though she belittled what she regarded as an unacceptable infu-
sion of political ideology into his social science. Sutherland, Kornhauser
maintained, tended to excuse the behavior of slum boys who become delinquent and to accuse the rich of abominations. Falling prey to what might be
regarded as overblown rhetoric, she argued that Sutherland's stand on
white-collar crime was "a luxury affordable only by professors who, in the
safety of their studies, are immune to the consequences of grimy-collar
crime."[89] The people from whom Sutherland derived many of his ideological
ideas were not academics but rather farmers on the Midwestern prairie. Besides, the term "grimy-collar" may be seen as condescending to persons in a
social class below Kornhauser's. In addition, rather than being insulated, a
number of academics have been victimized by street crimes—the death toll
of professors from acts of discontented students is not insignificant; neither
is the mugging rate with professor victims in urban-center universities such
as Chicago, Columbia, and the University of Southern California.

Despite his youthful immersion in populist doctrine, nothing in
Sutherland's earlier criminological work would have prepared his audience for his biting indictment of upper-world criminals, though there
were signposts along his scholarly path that might well have implanted the
subject in his subconscious. Cesare Lombroso, often designated the father
of criminology (Sutherland is likely to be called the "father of American
criminology"), despite his exaggerated attention to biological traits as the
root cause of crime, had a number of things to say about what would
become known as white-collar crime: "The statesman who wishes to prevent crime ought to . . . guard against the dangerous effects of wealth no
less than against those of poverty," Lombroso wrote.[90] He went on to pinpoint an ugly side of politics:

[P]olitical power is obtained, no longer at the point of a sword, but by money; money is extracted from the pockets of others by tricks and mysterious maneuvers, such as the operation of the stock exchange. The commercial warfare is carried on . . . through the perfection of the art of deceit, the skill acquired in giving the purchaser the impression that he is getting a good bargain.[91]

Nor was Lombroso done with this subject. He went on to write about what he called "latent criminals," employing an adjective favored by Freud when he wrote about "latent homosexuality":

Still less different from born criminals are those latent criminals, high in power, whom society venerates as its chiefs. They bear the marks of congenital criminality, but their high position generally prevents their criminal character from being recognized. Their families, of which they are the scourges, may discover it; or their depraved nature may be revealed all too late, at the expense of the whole country, at the head of which their own shamelessness, seconded by the ignorance and cowardice of the majority, has caused them to be placed.[92]

Much nearer to home, Charles Richmond Henderson, the university chaplain and Sutherland's graduate advisor at the University of Chicago, believed that "the scholar's duty is to aid in forming a judicial public opinion as distinguished from the public opinion of a class and its special pleadings."[93] Sutherland had enrolled in the divinity school at Chicago but was persuaded by the professor with whom he had taken a correspondence course in order to qualify for graduate school admission to sign up for Henderson's class called "Social Treatment of Crime." Henderson offered the following observations about white-collar crime in the textbook that has been credited with founding the academic study of crime and deviance:[94]

The social classes of the highest culture furnish few convicts, yet there are educated criminals. Advanced culture modifies the form of crime, tends to make it less coarse and violent, but more cunning; restricts it to quasi-legal forms. But education also

opens up the way to new and colossal kinds of crime, as debauch-
ing of conventions, councils, legislatures, and bribery of the press
and public officials. The egoistic impulses are masked and dis-
guised in this way, the devil wearing the livery of heavenly char-
ity for cloaks of wrong. Many of the "Napoleons" of trade are well
named, for they are cold-blooded robbers and murderers, utterly
indifferent to the inevitable misery which they might know will
follow their contrivances and deals.[95]

Henderson at first paid personal attention to Sutherland. "He spoke
to me, was interested in me. Consequently I was interested in pursuing
sociology, and interested in the type of sociology that Professor Henderson
presented."[96] But in time, Sutherland grew disenchanted with Henderson,
and in a letter to a fellow graduate student, he wrote sarcastically that
when he finished his Ph.D. dissertation on unemployment in Chicago he
hoped Henderson "will not read it any more thoroughly than he reads
the books he reviews."[97]

Albion Woodbury Small, the founding chair of the sociology department at Chicago, and still its head when Sutherland studied there, was no
less condemnatory than Henderson of America's large business enterprises: "Corporations are presumptively servants, not masters of the
public," Small wrote. "A corporation which is deficient in the discharges
of its delegated function should be restored to usefulness by vigorous
methods, if necessary, just as the proper public authority should repair a
bad road." Small went on to maintain that "the popular mind is at present
tending to the view that capitalistic organizations are inherently and
necessarily evil. Innumerable corporations are acting on the presumption
that the public is a mine, to be worked for all it is worth until the lead runs
out." The solution that Small offered was that "government should take
over some corporations who are antisocial."[98]

Sutherland's academic interests at Chicago had turned to Thorstein
Veblen, a renowned social economist, who had passed the biting judgment that the ideal captain of industry was like the ideal delinquent "in his
unscrupulous conversion of goods and persons to his own ends, and in a
callous disregard of the feelings and wishes of others and of the remoter
effects of his actions."[99] But Veblen left the University of Chicago to take a

position at Stanford University before Sutherland could study with him. Instead he signed up with Robert Hoxie, a labor historian and Veblen protégé, of whom he would later say that he "exerted more constructive influence in determining my thinking than did any of the sociologists."[100] In a book on trade unionism, Hoxie indicated the way he sought to teach his students to think:

> Most students will have to guard against the tendency to feel that a thing is good because it is the established, legal, ethical, or social thing. Some will have to guard against the tendency to feel that a thing is good because it is revolutionary or iconoclastic. Everyone must school himself to the view that nothing is absolutely right or sacred; that everything is open to examination and is to be judged solely by its effects. That is, it is for each one to put aside inherited and group prejudices as far as possible, and, imbued solely by the scientific spirit to search patiently for truth.[101]

"I would rather have a paper that showed one flash of real insight than the most elaborate and finished piece of copying or mere stringing together of information," Hoxie proclaimed. "Think out the meaning of things," he told students.[102] Perhaps it was from Hoxie that Sutherland derived the ideal of intellectual honesty that is reflected in his classic 1924 textbook when he observed: "The fundamental difficulty in the prevention of crime . . . is that no one knows definitely what should be done to prevent it."[103]

More contemporaneous with Sutherland, Albert Morris, a criminologist at Boston University, writing slightly before Sutherland's presidential address, pointed a critical finger at those he labeled "criminals of the upperworld," persons "whose social position, intelligence, and criminal technique permit them to move among their fellow citizens virtually immune to recognition and prosecution as criminals."[104] And, as we shall see in the next chapter, many voices, often lonely and largely unheeded, throughout the history of Western civilization have bewailed what Sutherland came to designate as white-collar crime.

Less certain, but intriguing, is the influence of his graduate students on Sutherland's focus on white-collar crime. He had scrawled on the first page of the manuscript of his presidential address: "Written by Mary Bess Owen, read by Edwin H. Sutherland, and listened to by Lois Marie Greenwood, when she wasn't thinking about something else." Owen and Greenwood, both sociology graduate students, were roommates at Indiana. Owen, twenty-four years old at the time, was in her first year in the doctoral program.

More than half a century later, I endeavored to learn what Sutherland meant by that note. Mary Owen Cameron was then quite sickly and confined to a wheelchair. She and her husband were living on the seventeenth floor in a New York University apartment at Washington Square. Her husband, English-born Kenneth Neill Cameron, a retired NYU professor, was a highly regarded scholar of the English poet Percy Bysshe Shelley and an ardent Communist who had written an admiring biography of Stalin.[105]

In an obituary notice—she died in 1998—Albert K. Cohen, a fellow Indiana graduate student, described Mary Owen Cameron as a person who "stood out for her brilliance, the force of her personality, and her contribution to the enterprise in which we were collectively engaged." Cohen noted that she would be remembered in many ways, but that "most will share the memory of her irreverence for authority and independence of character."[106] After leaving Indiana, she taught from 1952 to 1964 at Finch College in New York City, which she described to me as a "fashionable place for the stupid daughters of the very rich," and then taught for twenty-five years in the Department of Educational Foundations at Hunter College in the City University of New York system. It was obvious that she had been a striking young woman—and was still very handsome. She described Sutherland as about six feet tall, clean-shaven, good-looking, well-built, and noted that "he walked really easily, not rigid." Cameron recalled that what remained of Sutherland's hair was graying and was combed neatly to both sides of his head, and that he wore thin rimless glasses. She said she admired Sutherland "enormously" and believed then, and still did, that his outstanding trait was "integrity." But, she added, "Edwin was not a courageous man in every sense of the word. He was a cautious guy whose heart was in the right place. He tried not to cause trouble." He was "scared" that his polemics about white-collar crime might discredit his university, and that the fallout could hurt his personal life and his professional career. She thought that was why he so easily caved in to the demand of the Dryden Press that he eliminate the identities of the lawbreaking corporations.

Sutherland was only joking, Ms. Cameron told me, when he wrote those remarks on the manuscript. But she maintained that she herself was a "risk taker," "a deep-seated rebel," perhaps, she believed, as a rebellion against her rigidly conservative father, and that she had been influential in impelling Sutherland to castigate upper-class crooks. Her mother—Mary Bess was an only child—had worked in the circus, the woman who was "shot" out of a cannon into a far net (actually she was ejected by a rubber sling while a gun went off and smoke was emitted from the cannon). Mary Bess had been "ashamed" when she learned that her father was in the Ku Klux Klan. She described herself as "headstrong" and having "a rebel streak."[107]

I presumed that Ms. Cameron was inflating considerably her importance to the classic Sutherland paper. But when her husband left the room for a moment, she turned to me, smiled mischievously, and said: "You should know that I slept with Edwin nightly." Before I could ask any questions, Kenneth Cameron returned; it obviously was not appropriate to pursue *that* matter any further. My presumption is that by "nightly" Ms. Cameron meant during the course of the meetings in Philadelphia. Later, several of Sutherland's colleagues verified Mary Bess's story, though they had had no intention of telling me about it when they had discussed Sutherland with me earlier.

Mary Bess and Sutherland later had a falling out when she began dating her husband-to-be, who then taught in the Indiana English department, and she adopted his extreme left-wing views. She wrote her dissertation under the supervision of Karl Schuessler. It was later published as *The Booster and the Snitch* (1964) and remains a particularly highly regarded study of shoplifting, based on work at Chicago's Marshall Fields emporium.[108]

In a telephone interview from her home in Kent, Connecticut, Lois Greenwood Howard echoed Mary Bess Cameron's report on the meaning of the manuscript notation. She described Sutherland as "very handsome" and "extremely neat" and told how, when later in her life, she needed a Ph.D. to qualify for a particular job, Sutherland gave her his field notes on frontier banditry "and practically wrote the dissertation for me."[109]

Donald Clemmer, a noted scholar of prisons,[110] later claimed that a good deal of the credit for Sutherland's focus on white-collar crime should have gone to Ben Reitman, a medical doctor, and one of the most colorful figures ever to cross paths with the criminological community.[111] Reitman is best remembered as the lover of the brilliant and famous radical Emma Goldman (as well as a considerable number of other women during the same time). He occasionally lectured to Sutherland's classes. A committed hobo, Reitman often hopped freight trains for jaunts throughout the country and was known as the "clap doctor" for his dedication to providing treatment to the city's prostitutes for venereal infections.[112] While Reitman's vigorous championship of many of Goldman's critiques of American business likely had an impact on Sutherland, it seems far-fetched to credit him with any more than perhaps stoking the latent blaze of indignation that marked Sutherland's work.

Despite his hesitation and anxiety regarding difficulties that might ensue because of his attack on powerful forces in American life, Sutherland remained largely unscathed personally. When I obtained his FBI file through the Freedom of Information Act, it showed that the Bureau had ignored his ideological stance on white-collar crime except for one relatively inconsequential matter. That incident involved the invitation of J. Edgar Hoover, who later served for forty-eight years (1924–1972) as the fearsome head of the FBI, to address the first meeting of the National Institute of Mercenary Crime (NIMC). The group had been founded in Chicago in 1931 by Ernest MacDougall, a local lawyer of no particular prominence.[113] Sutherland, at the time a research professor at the University of Chicago, was the Institute's vice president when Hoover was invited to speak at the group's first meeting. Hoover had the special agent in charge of the Chicago FBI office look into the NIMC and MacDougall. The report indicated that MacDougall had a small balance in his bank account and a nondescript record as an attorney. The NIMC Board of Trustees, which included Sutherland, was said to "consist of men who are highly respected and very prominent in Chicago." The agent added: "It would appear, however, that most of them are educators and sociologists." The "however" in that sentence likely was the result of the agent's awareness of Hoover's biases. "He was suspicious of the academic community, of any intellectual—of any scholar," a biographer of Hoover has noted. "He disliked them instinctively."[114] Hoover politely declined the invitation.

Much more significant to the FBI were three talks by Sutherland in the spring of 1938 on successive days in Anderson, Fort Wayne, and LaPorte, all Indiana sites. In the presentations, Sutherland challenged, rather mildly, Hoover's claims that parole boards were returning "a den of rattle-snakes" from prisons to the street [115] A reporter for the *Indianapolis Times* sent a copy of the speech to the FBI with the result that Sutherland was placed on the Bureau's "no-contact" list and no longer was sent the agency's crime statistics report. When Sutherland wrote a letter of complaint, Hoover scrawled on it: "No answer." Later, Sutherland tried the office of the US senator from Indiana to secure the statistical report. Ultimately, the FBI reviewed Sutherland's dossier, and Clyde Tolson, Hoover's alter ego in the Bureau, wrote: "I suggest we now give him the *Uniform Crime* statistics only. His old parole cohorts have been pretty well licked." Hoover's verdict, penned below Tolson's memorandum, was: "Place him on list for crime reports from now on. No need to send him back issues. Need not acknowledge his letter." [116]

Despite his strong support of government control of gasoline consumption during wartime, Sutherland fundamentally was an advocate of free enterprise and was not in favor of radical social change, contrary to the assertion by law professor Leonard Orland, who insisted that "Sutherland's approach was Marxist criminality [and] was based primarily upon the socio-economic status of the offender." [117] Sutherland believed that the government had to regulate economic affairs in order to maintain capitalistic conditions of fair competition. Otherwise, corporations would engage in cutthroat predatory activity to the disadvantage of consumers. What Orland meant, one presumes, is that white-collar crime was in line with the strictures against the grand bourgeoisie that suffused the writings of Karl Marx. The Marxist label could just as insensitively be attached to studies that focus on lower-class criminals (or the *lumpenproletariat*, as Marx labeled them). Sutherland's personal economic position is set forth in a paragraph in an unpublished article about the A & P food stores:

> Free enterprise can be maintained in a society only if the economy is controlled by free and fair competition. When free and fair competition breaks down, the society must control by legislation either in the form of regulation or of public ownership.

> A & P is an illustration of the corporations which have grown big because of profits acquired illegally If the illegal practices of this corporation continue and expand, they will ruin the independent grocers. . . . A & P has obtained its position of 25 percent of the grocery trade in many communities. . . . They may raise their sights to 40 percent or 60 percent and then expand to other communities. This would be similar to socialism except that the public would have no voice in the industry. . . . A & P is driving the United States away from free enterprise into a socialistic economy.[118]

Sutherland's sympathy was for the small neighborhood grocer who was being forced out of business by a large supermarket chain, to the detriment of cozier, more personal shopping relationships that prevailed when he was growing up in Nebraska. But his rhetoric is overblown: A & P in time would be overshadowed by other supermarket giants, whose prices and variety of goods drew buyers away from local, generally higher priced food stores.[119] Socialism, neither in the form of state ownership nor in the nature of private monopolies, did not come to characterize the world of supermarkets, as Sutherland feared, though mergers of supermarket chains continue to be common.

Notwithstanding unending attempts to settle on a suitable definition, the term "white-collar crime" now enjoys widespread usage, and it has added a bite to commentaries about the illegal acts of businessmen, professionals, and politicians that is absent in blander designations, such as "occupational crime" and "economic crime," the latter the term of choice in Europe for such offenses, or "abuse of power," the term employed by the United Nations. In the Soviet Union, "economic crime" was the designation for offenses such as falsifying production totals and for dealing in the black market. Such acts were often considered to be treason against the state and severely punished, sometimes with death.[120] The difficulty with the term "economic crime" is that illegal acts committed for economic reasons cover a great deal of offending territory, perhaps most of it. Murder to inherit, arson to collect on an insurance policy, con games, and burglary and robbery—as well as numerous other crimes—are committed for economic reasons.

The term "abuse of power" also lacks a clear definitional foundation. Abuse of power can cover a very wide and problematic spectrum: it suffers from the absence of a link to substantive rules, such as those that define criminal activity. Was the invasion of Iraq by the United States an abuse of power? Is the striking of a child by a parent such an abuse? Should an affluent government with a high level of homelessness and hunger be regarded as abusing power?

The label "white-collar crime" has proven to be a felicitous ideological coinage. In terms of criminology a comprehensive survey found that Sutherland's *White Collar Crime* was regarded as the most significant contribution in the decade in which it appeared.[121] The original edition was translated in Japanese and Spanish and the uncut version into Italian.[122] The term itself has found its way in German criminology as *weisse-kragen kriminalitet*; into French as *crime in col blanc*; Italian as *crimen del colletti binachi*; Hebrew as *averot tzavaron halavan*; and Norwegian as *hvit krage-forbrytelse*, as well as other foreign renditions.

The ultimate tribute to *White Collar Crime* was accorded by Hermann Mannheim, who wrote: "There is no Nobel Prize yet for criminologists, and probably there never will be one, but Sutherland would have been one of the most deserving candidates for his work [on white-collar crime]."[123]

[2]

HISTORICAL PERSPECTIVES

The feral drive by persons in power for the accumulation of money by foul means has been characteristic of almost all civilizations at almost all times. "Men strive to outdo one another in every aspect of life," James Q. Wilson writes, "pursing power and wealth, pride and fame, beyond some reasonable measure."[1] Today, salaries are paid to corporate executives that Warren E. Buffett, the second richest person in the United States (Bill Gates of Microsoft is the richest individual in the country), paradoxically regards as "obscene."[2] These astronomic incomes typically are authorized by members of a board of directors that has been appointed by the corporate president. The perks, money, and stock options are, of course, perfectly legal, but they are deducted from company earnings that some would argue ought to be more equitably shared with stockholders and employees. The situation devolves into white-collar crime when an executive is unable to resist pressure to increase the businesses' earnings—at all costs, some of them illegal—to justify or escalate his or her salary.

Violations of criminal and civil law in commercial dealings also fly in the face of what is one of the less complicated definitions of morality: Do unto others what you would have them do unto you. This Golden Rule has been translated at times into corrupt business slogans such as the one enunciated by a tycoon after he took control of Pacific Lumber: "Those with gold, rule."[3] Another twist on common moral understanding was featured in a magazine cartoon showing a business executive informing an underling: "Honesty may be the best policy. But it isn't our policy." The dominant position through the ages that has marked the failure of the law to protect people against exploitation was expressed by an English judge in 1703. The case involved a man charged with obtaining money from a debtor by pretending that he was the agent of the man to whom the money was owed. The judge scornfully told the members of the grand jury: "Shall we indict one man for making a fool of another?" Both he and the jury members agreed that such an approach was not warranted.[4] The same judicial indifference appeared in another eighteenth-century case in which the defendant was charged with misrepresenting to a purchaser sixteen gallons of amber as eighteen gallons. "What is it to the public whether Richard Webb has, or has not, his eighteen gallons?" the judge declared.[5]

Morality and law are social constructs, and both in moral and legal terms white-collar crime is a good deal more ambiguous than violent street crimes. Stuart Green may be overstating the case, but he certainly is generally correct when he observes: "What is interesting and distinctive about [white-collar crime] is that, in a surprisingly large number of cases, there is a genuine doubt as to whether what the defendant was alleged to have done was in fact morally wrong." Green believes that part of the reason for this lies in the fact that white-collar offenses often are committed in the course of conduct that is otherwise legal and even socially productive.[6] The same, of course, is true of the crime of rape; and that is the reason why it often is so difficult to obtain convictions in cases in which rape is alleged.

Morality itself, particularly as it relates to law, is not necessarily a fixed concept that generates enduring public consensus, a matter clearly illustrated by shifting attitudes and changing statutes regarding behaviors such as homosexuality, abortion, gambling, and pornography.[7] The point is readily illustrated by debates prior to the Civil War regarding slavery. Ministers who saw themselves as thoroughly decent and scrupulously moral had no trouble defending slavery as an acceptable enterprise and quoted what they interpreted as relevant biblical passages to support their viewpoint.[8] White-collar crime is no exception to the rule that the definitions of the propriety of behaviors change as circumstances and values alter. Nonetheless, as we shall now see, voices throughout recorded times have been raised against white-collar crime, against the exploitation of the vulnerable by the powerful. The record shows that there has been a long-standing ancient tradition, passed on to the Judeo-Christian world, that associated commerce with fraud and avarice and that held that such endeavors were a potential source of moral corruption and decay. Objections also rested on a belief that commerce would lead to contacts with barbarian merchants, whose beliefs and practices challenged domestic orthodoxy.

STAVING OFF STARVATION

The historical record concerning access to food, essential for human survival, offers a template of attitudes and actions demonstrating the temper of particular times regarding a form of white-collar crime. Food shortages produced by climatic setbacks and severely aggravated by merchants seeking to take advantage of a seller's market have occurred throughout ancient history.

Greece

In the seventh century BCE, Solon, a leading Greek statesman and lawgiver as well as a poet, restricted the export of agricultural products, apart from olive oil, seeking to keep merchants from the free disposal of their goods to the highest bidder in times of dire need. Solon's edicts reflect the widespread hostility toward middlemen, who were seen as siphoning off money that should go to the person who had produced the product. The ideal was a face-to-face transaction between the farmer and the buyer. Solon's philosophy on morality and the market is reflected in one of his poems:

> *Often the wicked prosper, while the righteous starve;*
> *Yet I would never exchange my state for theirs.*
> *My virtue for their gold. For mine endures,*
> *While riches change their owner every day.*[9]

A decree issued about 476 BCE on the island of Teos, a Greek port on the west coast of Asia Minor, imposed a curse on malefactors that was to be read thrice yearly on a public occasion:

> If anyone prevents grain from being imported into the land of
> Teos by any pretext or device, either by sea or from the mainland,
> or forces up prices of imported grain, that man shall die both
> himself and his family.[10]

To have provoked a reaction of this kind, one writer observes, such conduct must have been common. In practice, the penalty that accompanied the curse—which could invoke deep fear itself—probably involved a ban against the wrongdoer trading in the marketplace, the Greek *agora*,[11] with the death penalty coming into play only after repeated transgressions. The

Greeks maintained that their legal codes had been delivered to them by the gods, but to avoid overly harsh results they would assume that they had received the laws imperfectly, that the expression of the will of the gods had been misinterpreted, so that changes could be made and justice done.[12]

Lysias, a renowned Greek orator in the fourth century BCE, wrote a speech that he put in the mouth of a prosecutor who was seeking to convince a jury to impose the death penalty on a hoarder of wheat. Hoarders, the prosecutor declaimed, thrive on the misfortunes of citizens such as those serving on the jury. They create rumors that ships carrying grain have been lost or that they have been captured by the Spartans, or that trading ports have been blockaded, or that a truce with Egypt's enemies is about to collapse. Malevolent merchants, the prosecutor argues, make massive profits out of these kinds of rumors and "prefer to risk their lives on a daily basis rather than to stop making unjust gains at your expense"[13]—for such transgressions carried a death penalty.

Flavius Philostratus, a Roman historian, tells the story of Appolonius, a heroic Greek figure who lived from 260 BCE to 190 BCE, visiting a remote site and finding the people on the verge of starvation. The populace was about to bury the island's governor alive; he clung desperately to the inviolable statue of the emperor. To save his life, he identified to the mob those who were hoarding grain. The miscreants were summoned and the governor read them Appolonius' message (Appolonius himself was fulfilling a vow of five years of silence). "The earth is the mother of all, for she is just," he had written. "But you because you are unjust have pretended that she is your mother alone; and if you do not stop, I will not permit you to remain on her." The hoarders were so terrified by this pronouncement that they filled the marketplace with grain and the population averted starvation.[14] More generally, Greek commercial crime is testified to by the fact that the Parthenon was built in the midst of bitter lobbying and in-fighting, and the architect had to flee Athens to escape charges of embezzlement.[15]

The Roman Empire

Rome relied heavily on foreign shipments for its grain supply, particularly shipments from Sardinia and Sicily, the latter the granary of the ancient world. Marketplace violations regarding grain remained a peripheral matter in the Roman world since grain was distributed by the Emperor to upward of 100,000 Roman citizens free of charge from the first century to near the end of the third. The aim was not humanitarian (need was not a requirement to receive a grain supply), but rather political—to keep the masses quiet. This tactic illustrates how at least certain forms of white-collar crime can be controlled, even eliminated, by measures that remove the need and the incentive for lawbreaking.

Roman law decreed that *dardanarii*, those who conspired to raise the price of grain, oil, bread, meat, or salt by the detention of vessels, the suppression of provisions, or similar practices, were to be fined. Specific laws focused on the honesty of magistrates who were charged with the supervision of the market; women and slaves were encouraged to provide evidence of any wrongdoing by these officials.[16]

Roman law foreshadowed today's suspicion of corporate entities. According to Edward Gibbon, the foremost historian in his time of the empire, Rome's rulers "viewed with the utmost jealousy and distrust any association among its subjects, and . . . the privileges of public corporations, though formed for the most harmless or beneficial purposes, were bestowed with a very sparing hand."[17]

Judeo-Christian Precepts

Actions and warnings against marketplace duplicity were common in early Judeo-Christian times. As two commentators observe: The Jewish prophets "bitterly attacked the luxurious lifestyles of the elite, their corruption, hypocrisy, immorality, injustice, and oppression of the poor."[18] In the King James translation of Proverbs (11:26) there is the admonition: "He that withholdeth corn [grain], the people will curse him: but blessing upon the head of him that selleth it." In the Deutercanonical biblical apocrypha, we hear a prophet proclaim that "a merchant shall hardly keep himself from doing wrong and a huckster shall not be freed from sin. . . . As a nail sticketh fast between the joinings of the stones, so doth sin stick close between buying and selling" (Ecclesiasticus 26:29, 27:2). St. Jerome echoed this view: *Homo mercator vix aut nunquam potest Deo placere*: a man who is a merchant can seldom please God.[19] The same theme has echoed throughout the ages. As one of innumerable examples, Pope Pius XI in 1931 wrote: "The worst injustices and frauds take place beneath the obscurity of the common name of a corporate firm."[20]

Talmudic law also condemned marketplace immorality in the early Jewish settlements:

> ... for commodities which are deemed necessary to life such as wine, oils, and various types of flour, the Rabbis did not allow one to make profit as a middleman. These essential products were to be sold directly to the consumer in order to keep prices low.... The Talmud excoriated those who hoarded food in order to resell it at high prices, tampered with weights and measures ... and raised prices unjustly.[21]

Jewish theology summed up the importance of impeccable commercial ethics by declaring that the first question a person would be asked in the hereafter during judgment was: "Hast though been honest in business?"[22] A sixteenth-century rabbi compared money to fire in that one could not do without it, yet should not get too close to it.[23] In ancient Jewish and Germanic law, economic offenses were viewed as more serious than many crimes of violence. It was a Hebrew belief that those who committed their crimes in secrecy thought themselves not to be watched by God, and that therefore they should be punished all the more severely.[24] The German tribes regarded stealing as more serious than most crimes against the person because it was premeditated. They punished theft with death, while allowing fines to be paid for maiming and murder.[25] The same position was taken by the Italian poet Dante Alighieri, perhaps the greatest literary figure of the Middle Ages. In The Divine Comedy, Dante called fraud the true vice. John Noonan, Jr., a federal judge, has observed that Dante decreed fraud to be worse than violence, that "God's penology is unlike that of human courts, [which] generally tend to punish most severely those who have used force."[26] In Dante's blueprint of hell, white-collar criminals occupy a nethermost position. He wrote:

> *Fraud more displeases*
> *God*
> *And therefore the fraudulent*
> *Are the lower, and more pain*
> *Assails them.*[27]

These precepts on rare occasions have been translated into action. In Rome, as one instance, senators were bound by stricter laws because they enjoyed a higher status and received greater privileges. The Bible (Luke 12:48) preached that "unto whomsoever much is given, of him shall much be required." But, as Barbara Tuchman has wryly observed of early reformist prophets—Ralph Nader is a good contemporary example—scolding and passion have a tendency to grow tiresome.[28]

The difficulty involved in fashioning a criminal code that outlawed matters about which astute thinkers disagreed is illustrated by an example from the ancient and Middle Ages periods when a prominent Catholic Church authority took issue with the stance on marketplace maneuvers that had been advocated centuries earlier by one of Rome's leading orators. Saint Thomas Aquinas, writing in the thirteenth century, retold Cicero's observation in *De Officiis* (On Duties) about a merchant carrying grain from Alexandria to Rhodes, which had been stricken by famine. The merchant knew that others were following him with more grain. Was he bound to tell the townspeople about the additional grain, or might he remain silent and command higher prices? Cicero concluded that a moral obligation demanded disclosure.[29] Aquinas, however, granted that it would be commendable to tell, but he insisted that the merchant was not morally required to predict a future event since if the event failed to occur he would be robbed of a just price.[30] Philosopher Thomas Donaldson, recounting this difference of opinion, notes its tie to contemporary laws that demand that insiders share what they know and not employ the information for personal gain.[31]

Religious leaders in England later would echo the early theological concerns with cheating in business. The influential preacher William Perkins had particularly harsh things to say about grain hoarders and malevolent businessmen whose great desire for lucre led them to exploit their fellows.[32] John Bunyan, whose *Pilgrim's Progress* for a considerable period of time was outsold only by the Bible, raged against "every man that makes a prey of his advantage upon his neighbor's necessities, to force from him more than in reason and conscience, according to the present price of things, more than such commodity is worth, may very well be called an extortioner, and judged for one that hath no inheritance in the Kingdom of God." Such people, Bunyan proclaimed, "ought to be hissed out of the world."[33] Bunyan was echoing the dictate of the religious catechism of the time in which the question was posed to communicants: "May a man command beyond its worth what he is about to sell?" with the expected answer being: "No."[34]

Many writers of the times echoed these theological fulminations. Thomas Hobbes, a preeminent political philosopher, in a famous blast, found an unsavory comparison between corporations and parasitic ascarides; corporations, Hobbes declaimed, were "like worms in the entrails of natural man."[35] Daniel Defoe, the famed author of *Gulliver's Travels*, was "voicing established opinion"[36] when in an early seventeenth-century publication he commented that "there are frauds in trade with which tradesmen daily practice and which notwithstanding, they think are consistent with being honest men."[37] Christopher Hill offers an assemblage of scathing seventeenth-century criticisms of predatory profiteers, including, "With the superfluidity of his usury he built a hospital and harbors there those whom his extortion had spoiled; so while he makes many beggars he keeps some." Another critic sarcastically had a businessman saying, "I love churches. I mean to rob my countrymen, and build one."[38] In America, Edward Bellamy, seeking to portray what would be the characteristics of a utopian society, forbad commerce within its boundaries; no money and no trade was to be permitted.[39] More recently, the widely read English moral philosopher C. S. Lewis launched this broadside:

> The greatest evil is not now done in those sordid "dens of crime" that Dickens loved to paint. It is not done even in concentration camps and labor camps. In those we see its final result. But it is conceived and ordered (moved, seconded, carried, and minuted) in clean carpeted, warmed and well-lighted offices, by quiet men with white collars and cut fingernails, and smooth-shaven cheeks who do not need to raise their voices. Hence, naturally enough my symbol for Hell is something like the bureaucracy of a police state or the office of a thoroughly nasty business concern.[40]

While prominent theological thinkers fumed about white-collar transgressions, there were also those who placed the blame for such behavior squarely on the religious leaders themselves for what was said to be their failure to inculcate in their parishioners the moral standards that stood at the heart of their faith. John Ruskin, a nineteenth-century litterateur, for instance, expressed his indictment in these terms: "It is only through the quite bestial ignorance of the Moral Law in which English Bishops have contentedly allowed their flocks to be brought up, that any of the modern English conditions of trade are possible."[41]

FORESTALLING, REGRATING, AND ENGROSSING

Early English law, rooted in Roman edicts and the practices of the invading Saxons, Danes, and Normans, decreed that any person who conducted business had to bring witnesses before the king's deputy, who could testify to the details of the transaction and report when the business had been concluded. William Illingworth, writing in 1800, offered a summary of the regulations that prevailed in England in the years around 1100:

> No person shall buy, sell, bargain for, or exchange any cattle, cloth, or other commodity, except in the public market within the gates of cities and towns, in the presence of the port-reeve, town-reeve, king's reeve, or shire reeve [all were local officials], or a priest or an ordeler,[42] and in the most frequented and open part of the market and that such sales should not be made unless before witnesses, and with surety and warranty.[43]

In the thirteenth century these rules were enacted into statutes that outlawed three specific marketplace maneuvers: forestalling, engrossing, and regrating. Broadly defined, the triumvirate comprehended endeavors that sought to artificially raise the price of commodities, including spreading false rumors, buying foodstuffs in the marketplace before the specified opening time, and buying and then selling the same article in the same market for a higher price. The regulations were not totally altruistic attempts to ease the plight of ordinary consumers; for one thing, out-of-market transactions, like some tax-avoidance schemes today, kept the king from getting what he believed was his lawful due. In their time, these rules were the leading form of regulation, and they represent precursors of current regulations to control business practices.[44]

The first English Parliament, organized in 1266, enacted the initial statute outlawing forestalling. It is notable that women, the widows of earls and barons who had been killed in battle and the wives of those taken prisoner, participated in that session. This enactment and most others thereafter were responses to attention-arousing crises, as is much white-collar crime legislation today—or, in Lord Bacon's words, they were passed "on the spur of the occasion."[45] The moral condemnation of marketplace malevolence can be gathered from the wording of a 1306 statute:

> No forestaller shall be suffered to dwell in any town, who mani-festly is an oppressor of the poor, and a public enemy of the country, who meeting grain, fish, herring or other things coming by land or by water to be sold, doth hasten to buy them before another; thirsting after wicked gain and by that means goeth about to sell the said things much dearer than he brought them, who cometh about merchant strangers that bring merchandise, offering them help in the sale of their wares, and informing them that they may sell the wares dearer than they meant to have done, and by such craft and subtlety deceiveth a whole town and a country.[46]

First-time offenders could have their products confiscated, repeat of-fenders might be sentenced to a term in the pillory, where they could be viewed and mocked by the townspeople. Three-time culprits could be im-prisoned until they paid a ransom for release. One more offense and the violator might be expelled from England.

The landmark statute against forestalling was enacted in 1552, con-solidating previous laws and court rulings. But there were subtle changes taking place in commerce at the time. No longer could the country farmer conveniently place his open sacks of grain on a stall during the scheduled market period and stand before them and await a customer: other things needed his time and attention. It also was becoming easier to transfer commodities from a site with a surplus to one in need. The provincial population was growing and inland trade, with its need of middlemen, was obvious. By 1640 buying outside the official market was becoming more common, usually occurring at inns and in warehouses.[47]

Nevertheless, the death knell of forestalling would not be rung for an-other two hundred years. Toward the end of the sixteenth century, the Privy Council decreed that food scarcity was not evidence of the hand of God, but was due to human laxity and greed. The Council issued the fol-lowing edict—the original spelling is kept to offer a sense of changes in the English language over the centuries that parallel alterations in what is regarded as acceptable and unacceptable white-collar behavior:

> There are seene and fownde a number of wycked people in condicions more lyke to wolves or cormorants than to naturall men, that doe most covetusly seeke to holde up the late great pryces of corne [wheat] and other victuells by ingrossing the same into theire private hands berganynge beforehand for corne, and in some parts for grayne growing. ... Against which fowle, corrupt fraude and malycious greediness there are both manie good lawes and sondry orders of late yeres given to all Justices [of the Peace].[48]

Finally, in 1767, after diverse Parliamentary investigations, it was concluded that the existing laws condemning forestalling, engrossing, and regrating were handicapping free trade, discouraging the growth of commerce, and enhancing the prices of products. All parliamentary enactments on the subject were repealed, though the common law prohibitions—the rules that had been in force before parliamentary statutes were enacted—remained operative until 1844. During the Revolutionary War in America, George Washington had his say about forestalling, observing that the Congress was in default in its duty to prosecute profiteers and forestallers who jacked up prices of supplies they sold the army. They were, Washington wrote, "pests of society," all of whom ought to be "hung in gibbets five times as the one prepared by Haman."[49] Haman, a biblical villain, had erected a 75-foot-high gallows to hang all Jews, beginning with a court adviser who had refused to bow down to him. Queen Esther discovered the plan and Haman was executed on the gallows he had constructed to hang others (Esther 3:7).

The case of John Rusby that erupted during the period between the repeal of the laws and the elimination of common law provisions regarding forestalling illustrates the intensity of reactions to food shortages. Rusby, a middleman, had been indicted in 1798 for regrating. The charge was that he had bought and resold oats in the same market on the same day. He was tried before Lord Kenyon in 1800. Kenyon's ringing summary to the jury emphasized what he believed to be the starvation of the poor caused by acts such as Rusby's. He told the jurors: "Gentlemen, a precedent made in a court of justice that will stem the torrent of such affliction to the poor is certainly useful to the public."[50]

Three of the most preeminent thinkers of the nineteenth century chimed in on the debate about forestalling. Their views indicate the controversy that often underlies efforts to put a damper on unfettered self-seeking behavior and the problematic nature of attempts to referee the use of power. In his monumental treatise, *The Wealth of Nations*, Adam Smith insisted that the regulation of trading in grain was "altogether unmerited." Smith's position was that left to its own devices, a free market will ensure that equity prevails. In times of shortages, the merchant will raise his prices to a level only as high as a sufficient number of purchasers are able and willing to pay. This will put "the inferior kind of people upon their thrift and good management." While there may be some shortages, the "dreadful horrors of famine" will not ensue. Smith compares "the popular fear of forestalling and engrossing" to the "popular suspicions of witchcraft," a comparison that seems rather odd. Witches were accused of diabolic acts that no human being could conceivably have performed, such as flying about on broomsticks,[51] but people did in fact starve to death during times of crop failures and exorbitant prices. Smith was indicting the forestalling laws in terms of conditions that no longer prevailed when he wrote, not those conditions that existed when the laws were established.[52]

Jeremy Bentham, a political philosopher, disagreed with Smith, and took the position that it was the obligation of a country's leaders to use the powers they possessed to advance the welfare of those they supposedly served. Bentham wrote:

> I have not, I never have, nor ever shall have, any horror, sentimental or anarchical, of the hand of government. I leave it to Adam Smith ... to talk of invasions of natural liberty, and to give as a special argument against this or that law, an argument the effect of which would be to put a negative on all laws. The interference of government is an event I witness with satisfaction and with much more than I should its forbearance.[53]

Finally, Edmund Burke, another renowned English political philosopher, sided with Adam Smith. "Of all things, an indiscreet tampering with the trade of provisions is the most dangerous," Burke wrote, "and is always worst in the time when men are most disposed to it, that is, in time of scarcity." Burke maintained that government actions to create a level playing field for the poor in the realm of agricultural products inevitably backfires: "The wheel turns around, and the evil complained of falls with aggravated weight on the complainant."[54]

The shortcomings of unfettered marketplace laissez-faire, despite the arguments by Smith and Burke, would become painfully apparent as one food crisis after another surfaced in current times, particularly on the African continent. At the same time, failure to monitor the quality of food and drug products has led to unnecessary deaths, and uninspected mines have collapsed and killed and maimed underground workers. The toll in human life and suffering has been too high and at times too dramatic to allow entrenched economic interests to operate unfettered, most notably as their power became so immense that they came to exert unchecked influence over political decisions, both domestically and throughout the global economy.

The importance of the early marketplace offenses in foreshadowing the antitrust movement in the United States, which began with the passage in 1890 of the Sherman Antitrust Act, is reflected in Congressional debates on the subject and in subsequent court decisions. During the debates one Congressman observed that "monopoly . . . is the sole engrossing to a man's self."[55] Others focused on the demise of forestalling to support their opposition to laws suppressing monopolies. Chief Justice Edward Douglass White of the US Supreme Court in a bit of what jurists called dictum, that is, comments that represent musings on the subject being adjudicated, insisted that the repeal of the forestalling laws demonstrated that "the statutes did not have the harmful tendency which they were presumed to have when the legislation concerning them was enacted."[56] White's observation would be perfectly accurate had he chosen to use the words "no longer had" in place of "did not have." Others have clearly recognized this fact: Luke Owen Pike notes that "the ancient laws . . . were enforced as being . . . the only available means of keeping down [the prices of] the necessities of life,"[57] while Hans Thorelli adds that much of the original confusion surrounding the reach of current antitrust law was "probably due to a lack of insight into legal history."[58]

This scan of history in regard to marketplace transactions indicates that throughout time business and commerce have been regarded warily. Enforcement agents and theologians have endlessly condemned and sought to put a damper on such behavior. Nonetheless, the press for morality to accommodate under certain conditions to the realities of power has often resulted the flourishing of unacceptable and questionable behavior. Must we inevitably be faced with transgressions against decent and legal standards because of the nature of the market, or are commercial sins and crimes the work of rotten apples and contemptible cormorants? That is, is white-collar crime an unalterable structural ailment of the capitalist ideology, or does it represent the failure of powerful and prominent human beings to behave decently because of their personal inadequacy?

The early Egyptian, Greek, Roman, and Judeo-Christian precepts as well as the regulations seeking to create a relatively level playing field in the English commodity marketplace can be seen as attempts at economic regulation that underlie current efforts to control the abuse of power. Medieval peasants refused to starve to death gracefully; their counterparts today rebel against smog, impure water, stock market swindles, and a host of other wrongs. At the same time, in earlier days the struggle to stay alive could be all-consuming. Work schedules left little time for the niceties of self-preservation. Education and literacy were limited. It took time and other resources before white-collar crime could command considerable attention from its actual and potential victims.

THE MUCKRAKERS

The more contemporary background against which the social scientific study of white-collar crime in the United States played out was epitomized by a review of the exposés by a cadre of writers known as muckrakers. The muckraking period in the United States lasted from about 1903 to 1912 and captured the public imagination because of its verve and shock value. "Pallid conservative writing," Louis Filler has observed, "could not compete with it for attention."[59]

During the muckraking period, crusading writers published some ninety books and more than 2,000 articles in mass-circulation magazines that recently had been made inexpensive by new techniques of printing and distribution. About a third of the writing was by a dozen leading figures, persons such as Ida Tarbell, David Graham Phillips, Upton Sinclair, and Lincoln Steffens.

The term "muckrake" had been coined by Arthur Dent, an English Puritan clergyman, in his devotional guide, *The Plain Man's Pathway to Heaven*, published in 1601, which by 1704 had gone through thirty-five editions.[60] Dent's book was one of the pitifully few possessions brought to her marriage by John Bunyan's first wife.[61] Subsequently convicted for his nonconformist preaching, and while in Bedford prison, Bunyan wrote the famous allegorical treatise, *The Pilgrim's Progress*. In it, Bunyan told of a man who was so preoccupied with his muckrake, gathering up the world's filth, that he failed to look upward at the celestial glories.

Centuries later, President Theodore Roosevelt, though generally friendly to reformers, appropriated from Bunyan the term "muckrakers" to decry the investigative writers. Roosevelt was reacting angrily to a series of articles by Phillips attacking members of the US Senate, five of whom were under indictment and a number of others under suspicion of illegal activities.[62] Roosevelt castigated "the man who never does anything else, who never speaks or writes, save of his feats with the muckrake." Such a person, Roosevelt insisted, speedily becomes "not a help to society, but one of the most potent forces for evil."[63]

Five years later, Roosevelt apparently sought to make amends, noting in a speech that "muckrakers who rake up so much that ought to be raked up deserve well of the community, and the magazines which published their writings do a public service." Nonetheless, Roosevelt retained some reservations: "But they must write the truth," he added, "and the service they do must be real."[64]

The muckrakers most usually put before the public mountainous details of corruption and deceit gleaned from official records. They particularly focused on close alliances between business and politics, and they often wrote in terms of scorn and indignation. Note, for instance, Thomas W. Lawton's diatribe:

> The public, accustomed to invest its money in the legitimate securities of the country, had time and again lost hundreds of millions without dreaming that they had been as ruthlessly robbed as though held up at pistol-point by highwaymen. The public imagined that the great capitalists . . . were noble and public-spirited gentlemen of the highest moral principles and of absolute integrity. They know today that many of them are reckless and greedy stock gamblers, incessantly dickering with the machinery of finance for their own private enrichment.
> I have stripped the veil from these hypocrites and exposed to all the world their soulless rapacity. I have let the light of heaven into the dim recesses of Wall Street in which these buccaneers of commerce concocted their plots.[65]

Some muckraking writers devoted years to meticulous research seeking to pinpoint the holdings and operations of the country's largest corporations. A particularly good illustration is the work of Ida Tarbell, who discovered that the Standard Oil Company controlled all but 10 percent of the country's supply of petroleum. Standard Oil would undersell rivals, even to the point of suffering temporary losses, cut off their supplies, or otherwise make it virtually impossible for them to conduct business. The company's surge to power, under the leadership of John D. Rockefeller, was relentless, as it deployed part of its huge profits into continually absorbing competitors and purchasing whatever resources were deemed necessary for its sensational level of prosperity.[66] Tarbell's reporting won fifth place on a list of the ten best pieces of journalism for the entire century.[67]

The work of Tarbell contributed to the passage of the Sherman Antitrust Act in 1890. Following two decades of inertia, the government finally used the Act, which outlawed monopolies and restraints of trade to bring Standard Oil to heel. The sheer complexity of the case mounted by the corporation lawyers provides a foretaste of the maneuvering practiced by skilled and highly paid attorneys working on behalf of business firms. The record before the United States Supreme Court bench in the Standard Oil case came to 12,000 pages, an outpouring of verbiage that Chief Justice Edward White described as containing "a vast amount of confusing and conflicting testimony."[68]

In their decision against Standard Oil, the judges explained why they believed that Congress had forbidden the kind of behavior that marked the company's business tactics:

> [The Congressional debates] conclusively show that the main cause which led to the legislation was the thought that it was required by the economic conditions of the time, that is, the vast accumulation of wealth in the hands of corporations and individuals, the enormous development of the corporate organizations, the facility for combination which such organization afforded, the fact that . . . the combinations known as trusts were being multiplied and the widespread impression that the power had been and would be exerted to oppress individuals and the public generally.[69]

Justice John M. Harlan joined with the majority but filed a partial dissent as well. Harlan was a fiercely independent jurist, best known today for having rendered the lone dissent in the notorious *Plessy v. Ferguson* decision that upheld the "separate but equal" doctrine in race relations. Harlan's dissent declared that the Constitution is "color-blind."[70] In the Standard Oil case, he believed that the court had not been tough enough in its condemnation of every restraint of trade rather than attempting to determine if some arrangements might be acceptable He added:

> All who recall the condition of the country in 1890 will remember that there was everywhere—among the people generally—a deep feeling of unrest. The Nation had been rid of human slavery—fortunately, as all now feel—but the conviction was universal that the country was in real danger from another kind of slavery that would result from aggregations of capital in the hands of a few individuals and corporations controlling, for their own profit and advantage exclusively, the entire business of the country, including the production and sale of the necessities of life. Such a danger was thought to be imminent, and all felt that it must be met firmly and by such statutory regulation as would adequately protect the people against oppression and wrong.[71]

Samuel McClure, the editor of *McClure's*, for a time the leading muckraking magazine, with a monthly circulation of half a million readers, explained that his writers were filling a vacuum largely created by the inertia and indifference of other social institutions. McClure put the matter bluntly. Capitalists, workingmen, politicians, and citizens, he claimed, all were breaking the law. Who was left to uphold it? Lawyers, McClure said, advised corporations on how to get around the law, judges relied on quibbles to free rich defendants, despite evidence against them that was overwhelming. Churches owned filthy, ill-tended tenement dwellings that they rented to the poor at exorbitant rates, and academics really did not understand what was occurring in the world outside their ivied enclaves.[72]

The demise of the muckraking movement not long after the beginning of the second decade of the twentieth century carries instructive lessons. Part, but only a minor part, of the decline of muckraking resulted from effective pressures exercised against the muckraking magazines by the forces they were attacking.[73] Wounded corporations ceased advertising and, even more effectively, purchased some of the muckraking publications. Much more significant was a growing tendency toward sensationalism and shrillness as the magazines, having mined the most promising subjects, became more frantic about outdoing competitors and capturing public attention. The public, for its part, apparently became bored with what seemed to be an incessant diet of social criticism.

Muckraking had virtually disappeared when the advent of World War I conclusively turned citizens' attention to international concerns. The summary judgment by Cornelius Regier does not seem unreasonable: "Muckraking, however necessary and however valuable it might have been for the time being, was essentially a superficial attack upon a problem which demanded—and demands—fundamental analysis and treatment."[74] It was now emphasized that what was happening in the upper echelons of American organizational life was not the product of a few bad apples in an otherwise untainted barrel but had to be understood as the product of rampant economic and political conditions. This is not to say that individual villains at whom citizens might hiss were not identified. Ida Tarbell, with her mixture of cold disdain and white-hot indignation, for instance, painted a picture of a reptilian John D. Rockefeller, who "slithers" through the pages of her Standard Oil history.[75]

In today's society, the role of muckrakers has been assumed by investigative reporters who generally work for the nation's largest newspapers. It reached its zenith when Carl Bernstein and Bob Woodward fed the public details of the Watergate burglary during the presidency of Richard Nixon.[76] The stories were so revelatory of wrongdoing that Nixon was forced to resign rather than face what likely would have been a successful impeachment process. Woodward continues his probes today though the results are tamer since he cannot afford to alienate powerful political figures who offer him special access to their thoughts and documents. His goal remains to uncover what he calls "holy shit" stories; that is, information that will cause readers to so exclaim when they are confronted with what he has learned.[77] In addition, a muckraking role has been assumed by whistleblowers, who typically are strategically placed employees who, for a variety of reasons, feel impelled to report the wrongdoings of their organization to the media or to enforcement authorities. It is noteworthy that the 2004 cover of *Time* magazine, recognizing the most significant Person(s) of the Year, featured a trio of whistleblowers, all women, who worked in different settings and had reported wrongdoing in those workplaces.

Television, on occasion, particularly in widely viewed network programs such as *60 Minutes*, carries muckraking material, but it is difficult for it to portray complicated transactions vividly and in a compelling manner. A common tactic is to thrust a microphone in the face of an alleged white-collar offender and ask a question that might surface in an intense courtroom cross-examination. If the target refuses to answer, sometimes swatting the microphone aside, the implication is that his or her "rudeness" implies guilt. The advantage of television coverage is that it reaches so wide an audience and thereby can sway public policy.[78]

Public interest groups devoted to oversight activities constitute another prominent post-muckraking-era force. "Scratch the image of any industry and unsavory practices become visible," claims Ralph Nader, using language that echoes that of Edwin Sutherland.[79]

[3]

CORPORATE CRIME

The front pages of American newspapers today, when they are not displaying pictures of dead bodies lying about on Middle East killing fields and in African refugee compounds, are likely to show a corporate executive in a business suit with handcuffs on his wrists that are pinioned behind his back. The business big wheel is being taken into custody or led into a criminal court by government agents wearing orange jackets with large letters on the back that identify their agency affiliation. This development differs dramatically from earlier days when news of a business leader who had been charged with a criminal act (unless it was a sex scandal) was likely to be buried in the paper's business section, if it was attended to at all. The offender of that era also was most likely to be treated in a gentle and respectable manner by law enforcement personnel.

The altered behavior by enforcers against corporate wrongdoers—and the dramaturgy of such efforts—is one of the more significant developments in the arena of corporate crime. Its purpose is almost exclusively symbolic. There is no sensible reason to raid the house of a corporate executive in the middle of the night to arrest him or her, and there is no real purpose served by handcuffing and inviting media photographers to snap pictures of the businessman or businesswoman being hauled into court. The aim is to humiliate, an arguable tactic at best, and to demonstrate vividly that felons in the suites deserve no better treatment than those in the streets. An upper-class suspect occasionally will seek, usually with little success beyond self-satisfaction, to beat federal agents at their own game. Jeffrey Schilling, allegedly Enron's mastermind offender, refused to wear a tie or belt when he was arrested, saying that he would not give those taking him into custody the satisfaction of confiscating these items.

The dramatized arrest scenarios have another purpose as well. The desire to focus attention on what they are accomplishing is one of the prime goals of American regulatory agencies. They live (and sometimes die) in terms of public perceptions of the success of their activities, matters that become of prime importance during Congressional hearings on their budget request for the forthcoming fiscal year. This consideration at times creates a dilemma for agency heads: should they pursue a large number of small business firms, where the going is easier, or should they undertake the considerably more formidable task of taking on a few giant corporations? The first strategy yields a much larger number of "success" stories; the second will grab headlines but reduce significantly the total number of prosecutions that can be heralded before an inquiring congressional appropriations committee. It was the finely tuned bureaucratic instincts of J. Edgar Hoover in regard to such considerations that led the FBI under his direction to ignore organized and white-collar crime in order to ring up an impressive total of solved auto thefts and to claim credit for recovery of the total amount of the value of the vehicles they located.

This chapter considers some of these characteristics of corporate crime in the United States, a matter that is largely handled by federal agencies. The relation between law enforcement and the world of business is marked by numerous subtleties. Election to federal office (and the concomitant power to control enforcement agencies) is heavily dependent upon money contributed by those who have it to spare and who anticipate gains from its donation—most notably persons in the upper echelons of the corporate world and the entities they represent. Typically, presidents and members of Congress will endorse punitive actions against harmful business practices if it becomes necessary to do so to remain in office, that is, to placate constituents. Even then, they often will wield a symbolic big stick that is fashioned of straw. Only when public concern or outrage appears likely to dislodge them from their power positions will they, however reluctantly, support effective punitive measures against their financial benefactors. This is most likely to occur when there is a sickening tragedy that can reasonably be related to commercial malfeasance: deaths due to drugs that were approved on the basis of fraudulent tests, uninspected mine shafts that collapsed and killed dozens of miners. An appreciation of this situation is essential for an adequate understanding of the doctrine of corporate crime as it has come to be formulated and enforced in the United States.

THE BACKGROUND

Corporate criminal liability builds on the legal fiction that a corporation can be transformed by some alchemic verbal slight of hand into a human being with no affront to logic and no abuse of common sense. A corporate entity has no soul to damn and no body to kick, Edward, the first Baron Thurlow, observed in the nineteenth century.[1] The law in the United States has chosen to treat the corporation as if it were a human being, despite the fact that, among other matters, and unlike the rest of us, it has no limited span of existence on this earth and no corporeal substance that can be brought before a court.

The doctrine of corporate criminal liability is paradoxical and pragmatic. The paradox lies in the distinction between a corporate entity and all other entities that are exempt from liability for the criminal acts of their members. If the father in a family burglarizes a neighbor's house, no criminal charge will be framed in terms of the *State v. The Olivers*, with the accused being not only the particular violator but also the entire family that was accorded its identity by means of a state-granted license. This remains true despite Sir Henry Maine's statement that the family is a corporation and the patriarch (at least in Sir Henry's nineteenth-century century England) is the equivalent of what today would be the chief executive officer.[2] When war criminals are indicted by the victors (it is inevitably the victors who find themselves in a position to identify the losers' war criminals), it is individuals who are named, not nations. Otherwise, matters would become unmanageable. Nations are made up of a massive number of persons who contributed to an outcome in diverse and tangled ways, presuming that they have contributed in any way whatsoever. But corporations, though some in the United States have larger populations and more financial resources than many independent nations, are presumed to be more reasonably responsible for law violations than the people in a rogue country.

The pragmatism that underlies the doctrine of corporate liability in the United States includes the belief that corporate bodies have become so powerful that it is necessary at times to use the force of the criminal law— its potentially tough penalties and its ability to damage and destroy reputations—to deal with corporate malfeasance. The appraisal of corporate strength and dominance in economic life is reflected in the remark of a Congressman to a business executive during a committee hearing.

"Having this great economic concentration in your company," the Congressman stated, "you remind me of what somebody said before this committee some years ago. 'Every man for himself,' said the elephant as he danced among the chickens.'"[3] In addition, corporations typically possess deep pockets that can be made to disgorge monies to compensate those they have injured. Finally, the web of decision making inside a large institution often proves to be distressingly difficult to unravel in order to pinpoint a culpable wrongdoer. It can be much simpler to indict the entity, and, if things go well, culpable executives may be wont to cooperate in a corporate guilty plea rather than endure a courtroom battle, particularly if they can cut a deal that will preserve their own hides.

Corporate criminal liability in the United States finds support not only in juridical developments but also in philosophical observations that see a corporation as differing from its component human parts. It has been claimed that "a corporation has a personality of its own distinct from the personalities which compose it, a group personality different from and greater than . . . the sum of the parts."[4] This claim was reinforced with the observation that "in the same way that a house is something more than a heap of lumber and an army something more than a mob, . . . a corporate organization is something more than a number of persons."[5]

Corporate criminal liability is built upon a foundation of a deep distrust of the potential of free-ranging commercial power. That distrust over time has become increasingly manifest throughout the world in attempts to use the criminal law, which is viewed, though not necessarily altogether correctly, as the most potent weapon to control corporations and, at times, as a desperate last resort.

THE SOUTH SEA BUBBLE CASE

A crucial episode that triggered government efforts to control the exploitation of the public by corporate plundering took place in England almost 300 years ago. The South Sea Company was chartered in London in 1711 to accomplish two goals: first, to ease the backbreaking burden of a £10 million national debt by absorbing as stockholders those owed money by the government; second, to reward its shareholders with what its promoters claimed would be heady profits from the importation of slaves[6] and, more important, revenues from trade in what was called the "South

Seas," by which was meant South America from the Orinoco River to the south of Tierra del Fuego. The Scheme (as it was called) was wildly improbable from the outset. "It was wholly impossible it should have issued in anything but disaster," historian William E. H. Lecky would later observe.[7] The company prospered at first, primarily because huge bribes were slipped to members of Parliament to support it. It also flourished because English citizens with money enough to invest had no experience with the stock market from which to draw lessons. The Bank of England and the East India Company were the major stock issuers of the time[8] As of 1693, the latter had only 499 shareholders, with eighty-eight men owning three-quarters of the total stock. A brisk market in stocks only really began, though it increased with remarkable speed, after the incorporation of the South Sea Company.[9]

Stockholders continuously were misled about the true financial fortunes of the South Sea Company. Its share price surged wildly because of a snowball effect created by clever manipulation of the atmosphere surrounding the company and because of the greed of a public scenting huge profits. Managers of the stock made it easy to invest, allowing purchases for as low as 10 percent of the total value. Buyers presumed that they would be able to raise the funds that were due later merely by selling a small portion of the stock they were now purchasing at a magnificent profit.

A fierce speculative mania sent the price of South Sea stock on a ride that lasted almost a decade. When the stock came on the market in October 1711, it was quoted at between 73 and 76.[10] Near the end, on July 16, 1720, South Sea shares were selling at about 2,000, their highest level,[11] but by August of the same year they had dropped to 900 and forty days later had plummeted to 190.

Ironically, part of the company's difficulty was created by passage of the Bubble Act,[12] which had been urged by the South Sea Company directors. The success enjoyed by the South Sea investors had prompted the incorporation of myriad other enterprises, some of them with patently absurd promises, such as one that solicited funds to construct a perpetual motion machine.[13] The money these newer corporations were attracting reduced significantly the funds available for investment in the South Seas enterprise. The unexpected upshot was that when the other corporations went downhill they had to call for further money from those who had speculated on margin (that is, bought the stock by initially paying only a fraction of the total cost). This led to withdrawals from South Seas investments and endangered that company's financial condition.

Over the long run, until its repeal in 1825,[14] the Bubble Act inhibited the development of the corporation in England, and concomitantly, the emergence of a sophisticated body of law to establish the boundaries within which such organizations could operate.[15] King George I sounded a particularly loud blast against the South Sea Company when things began going sour, berating the speculative fever that he insisted was diverting folk from more practical pursuits, "taking off the minds of many of our subjects from attending to their lawful employments and by introducing a general neglect of trade and commerce."[16] Unfortunately for the King, two of his mistresses apparently had been bribed by Company directors, though this could not be proved conclusively because the official keeping the company books had fled overseas. "Self-preservation has compelled me to withdraw myself," he sensibly explained in a note he left behind.[17]

A Parliamentary inquiry found that 122 members of the House of Lords and 462 members of the House of Commons had invested in the Scheme. A major surprise was that there was no statute that allowed criminal proceedings to be launched against the malefactors. One Parliamentarian, who had lost a considerable sum, plunged into that gap by insisting, unsuccessfully, that the company directors should be declared guilty of parricide—that they had, in effect, murdered the country, their fatherland. If found guilty, he declared, they should receive the penalty decreed in ancient Rome by being sewn up in sacks with a monkey and a snake and cast into the river.[18] Ultimately, fines were imposed on those deemed guilty, some of them severe.[19]

The legislative oversight and inquiry that followed the South Seas Company disaster was very much like similar procedures today for the investigation of corporate crime. Such inquiries have the advantage of being able to uncover information that ordinarily is not available from court records because of procedural and evidentiary restraints. Nor is the data accessible to academics because of their lack of clout and, typically, their limited resources. Nobody has to respond to a question from a social scientist, but legislators can employ subpoenas and oaths and, at times, some highly skilled questioning tactics during investigatory hearings.

RAILROADS AND REFORM

The principle of corporate criminal liability, derailed for some time by the Bubble Act, developed slowly in the United States, which imported almost all of its body of law from England. It began inconspicuously, with regulations against boroughs and municipalities for such nonfeasance as failure to keep roadways clear and to attend to bridge repairs. Resistance to further expansion of corporate criminal liability rested on the nonhuman nature of the corporation. In a famous early Supreme Court ruling, Chief Justice John Marshall declared that the corporation was but "an artificial being, invisible, intangible, and existing only in contemplation of law."[20] Similarly, John Salmond, another preeminent legal figure, argued that "ten men do not in fact become one person because they associate themselves for one end, any more than two horses become one animal when they draw the same cart."[21] At the time, these positions were little more than debating points.

The first corporation in the United States was not organized until 1786, and by 1801 there still were only eight manufacturing companies in the country and only 317 corporations of all types.[22] Then came the railroads, swashbuckling across the country, killing unwary bystanders, setting fire to fields adjacent to their tracks, and using their extraordinary power to establish discriminatory and exorbitant haulage rates.

The railroads were America's first big business, and they made other businesses possible and necessary,[23] and "in one way or another, every new economic disruption that arose was related to the railroads and their practices."[24] The virtues and dangers of the railroad in the development of America has been summarized by legal historian Lawrence Friedman:

> It was the key to economic development. It cleared a path through the wilderness. It bound cities together, and tied the farms to cities and the seaports. Yet, trains were also wild beasts; they roared through the countryside, killing livestock, setting fires to houses and crops, smashing wagons at grade crossings, mangling passengers and freight. Boilers exploded, trains hurtled off tracks; bridges collapsed; locomotives collided in grinding screams of steel.[25]

The self-protective and manipulative actions of railroad corporations were aided by a 1896 Supreme Court decision that guaranteed them

protections granted citizens by the Fourteenth Amendment to the constitution,[26] with the prominent exception of the Fifth Amendment privilege
against self-incrimination.[27] The so-called railroad Robber Barons were
described as "cold-hearted, selfish, sordid men"[28] or, put another way, they
were said to be "scrupulously dishonest."[29]

After this and the proliferation of additional corporate entities, one
writer could observe: "Given the ubiquitous nature of corporations in our
society, economic and social considerations have preempted the importance of anachronistic theories and conceptual consistency."[30] More
simply put, it had become high time to rein in the corporate world.

The rapaciousness of the railroad corporations elicited a call for reform
from President Theodore Roosevelt in a 1905 message to Congress:

> The fortunes amassed through corporate organization are now
> so large, and vest such power in those that wield them, as to make
> it necessary to give to the sovereign—that is, the government,
> which represents the people as a whole—some effective power
> over their corporate use.[31]

It was against this background that the landmark court ruling in the
United States endorsing corporate criminal liability was enunciated in
1908. The issue before the court concerned the payment by a railroad
company of a rebate to the American Sugar Refining Company for shipments made from New York to Detroit. Such payments had been forbidden in 1903 by the Elkins Act, which declared that if corporate officers,
acting within the scope of their employment, gave rebates to customers,
the criminal offense could be imputed to the corporation itself. In its un-
successful appeal to the United States Supreme Court, the railroad company primarily relied on the claim that the punishment fell upon
shareholders who were unable to defend themselves in court. The judges
ignored this argument and asked rhetorically: if the authorities could not
punish the corporation (though the assistant traffic manager also was
convicted), how could they effectively deal with what they deemed a
harmful and impermissible way of doing business?[32]

The *New York Central & Hudson River* railroad case was the definitive
declaration of the legitimacy of the principle of corporate criminal liability in the United States, though the court was able to cite a dozen or so
prior rulings to buttress its conclusion, including what today stands as the

rather painful decision of the Supreme Court earlier that year that upheld the criminal conviction of Berea College in Madison County, Kentucky, for admitting black students along with whites in violation of Kentucky's racial segregation law.[33]

ENFORCEMENT PATTERNS

The most important push favoring corporate criminal liability came from the American Law Institute's Model Penal Code (MPC) in the late 1950s.[34] Though the Code writers had trouble justifying so unusual a variation from traditional criminal law precepts, they never seriously considered abandoning the principle and thereby unsettling what had become widespread precedents. There was, however, a dissenting voice among those commenting on the draft proposal: Glanville Williams, a Cambridge law professor, believed that it might have been preferable to reexamine the idea of corporate criminal liability anew rather than to endorse what had developed. "I know that the Reporter has told us that the whole trend of decisions is in favor of extending corporate liability," Williams observed, "but he has also told us . . . that the case is not well reasoned on fundamental policy and it seems to me that the judges have not looked where they are going."[35] Gerhard O. W. Mueller, in a critique that remains valid almost half a century later,[36] maintained that the endorsement of corporate criminal liability was ill advised because of the absence of empirical evidence regarding its utility. Mueller surmised that enforcement efforts would largely produce monetary fines that would be seen as ordinary business operating expenses and would increase the cost of products and services to consumers.[37]

Mueller, as well as most others writing before recent events, underestimated how strong a force the doctrine of corporate criminal liability could become under particular circumstances. As we will see later in this chapter, the prosecution of Arthur Andersen, a limited partnership with thousands of employees, drove the company out of business. And the subsequent conviction of Martha Stewart for perjury sent the stock in her company plummeting. Companies not particularly dependent upon their reputation for law-abiding behavior but who rely more on the quality and prices of their products, companies such as General Electric and Westinghouse, generally lose little if any prestige or business from criminal convictions for matters such as antitrust violations; but those whose image is intimately tied to a celebrity such as Martha Stewart or whose work, such as tax auditing, has to be seen as squeaky clean, can be beheaded by charges of financial chicanery.

The American Law Institute Code declared that a corporation may be criminally liable for offenses committed by agents acting within the scope of their employment and on behalf of the corporation if the legislature had clearly proscribed the alleged behavior. The rule was moderated by a due diligence clause that specified that criminal liability would not follow if "the high managerial agent having supervisory responsibility over the subject matter of the offence employed due diligence to prevent its commission."[38] This principle would be eroded in time so that any corporate employee, even if specifically warned to abstain from a particular illegal act, would render the corporation criminally liable if he or she nonetheless carried out the act. In the leading case, the president of the Hilton Hotel chain and the manager of the Hilton hotel in Portland, Oregon, both told a purchasing agent that he was not to threaten suppliers with loss of business if the suppliers did not contribute to a fund to promote tourism in Oregon. He nonetheless went ahead and did just that. The court upheld the criminal conviction of the Hilton corporation, insisting that Congress had intended to impose liability upon business entities for the acts of those to whom they chose to delegate their affairs in order to stimulate a maximum effort by owners and managers to assure adherence by their agents to the requirements of the law. In this case, the agent was acquitted; the corporation was convicted.[39]

A later case involved the federal Currency Transaction Report Act, which requires banks to report all withdrawals of more than $10,000. On thirty-one occasions James McDonough wrote multiple checks, each one for an amount under $10.000, but together totaling more than that amount. The Bank of New England was convicted of failure to obey the law, and its appeal claim that it had exercised due diligence was rejected by the trial judge whose instructions to the jury would be endorsed by the appellate court: "[I]f any employee knew multiple checks would require the filing of reports, the bank knew it, provided the employee knew it within the scope of his employment."[40]

The US Sentencing Commission, while promulgating a schedule of tougher sentences for corporate criminal activity in 1991, permitted judges to mitigate penalties if the entity could demonstrate implementation of policies and programs aimed at inhibiting the offense before it occurred. At first, such mitigation was not permitted if the crime was committed by more senior employees with managerial responsibilities, but this exception was eliminated when the Commission in early 2004 overhauled the organizational sentencing guidelines. The Commission originally had proposed longer possible sentences for corporations but retreated in the face of powerful business lobbying efforts.[41] In practice, however, relatively few corporate crime cases reach the trial and sentencing stages; settlements are very much more common.[42] The accused's awareness of the stringent mandatory penalties demanded by the sentencing guidelines often serves to induce negotiated guilty pleas.

That the penalties for corporate criminal acts are getting much tougher appears to be a consequence of the fact that the American middle class increasingly has become involved in stock transactions. At the turn of the present century, some 40–50 percent of Americans owned corporate shares compared to, for example, Germany, where only 5–7 percent of the people did so.[43] However empathetic you might be, it is one thing to hear of others who suffer losses because of illegal business behavior; quite another thing when you personally are the victim.

It is notable that in the United States regulatory agents typically (though by no means always, as we shall see in the initial case discussed later) adopt an adversarial stance, based on the assumption that a corporation will try to get away with everything it can,[44] while in England the attitude of inspectors tends to be that cooperation is the best way to achieve mutually desirable outcomes.[45] A "perverse effects" thesis takes issue with the tough American enforcement approach. It insists that such tactics create disincentives to report and to remedy corporate legal problems quickly rather than to fight the enforcement effort.[46]

The erratic nature of enforcement efforts in the United States can be seen in the two illustrative cases discussed next.

OCCUPATIONAL DANGER: THE MOEVES CASE

The irresponsibility of regulatory agents was painfully illustrated by an investigative newspaper reporter who examined the deplorable performance record of the Moeves Plumbing Company in Fairfield, Ohio, and the pusillanimous bureaucratic response of the federal Occupational

Safety and Health Administration (OSHA). The lead paragraph of the story sets the stage:

> As the autopsy confirmed, death did not come right away for Patrick M. Walters. On June 14, 2002, while working on a sewer pipe in a trench ten feet deep, he was buried alive under a rush of collapsing muck and mud. A husky plumber's apprentice, barely 22 years old, Mr. Walters clawed for the surface. Sludge filled his throat. Thousands of pounds of dirt pressed on his chest, squeezing and squeezing until he could not draw another breath.[47]

The OSHA law mandates training for persons who work in potentially dangerous digs so that they learn how to create safe conditions. There must be inspections by a "competent person" before work begins, sloping walls must be constructed, and a ladder and a metal box shield are required in excavations more than 5 feet deep. None of these provisions had been met in the Walters case, nor had they been in place in 1989 when another Moeves worker was buried alive under nearly identical circumstances.

OSHA law, severely emasculated by the business community when it was enacted, calls for criminal penalties only when there is a death that is caused by a willful violation of safety laws, meaning that the company demonstrated either "intentional disregard" or showed "plain indifference."[48] Linda Moeves had taken over Moeves Plumbing after her husband's death, and her unfamiliarity with regulations and her promises of reform had shielded the business from criminal liability in 1989; it received a $13,700 fine for the death of its employee at that time.

Efforts by the Walters family to secure a criminal prosecution as retribution for his death ran into endless blockades. First, OSHA had to define the neglect as "willful" and then it had to convince the Department of Justice to take on the case. Ultimately, OSHA issued a finding that Moeves had committed one "willful" violation by failing to provide protection against a collapse. But a day later the word "willful" was redacted and replaced by "unclassified," a term coined by corporate lawyers. It disallows criminal action though it carries heavier fines than a regular charge and requires an agreement to make significant safety improvements. Walters's father, saying that the government betrayed his son's memory, vowed to fight OSHA for the remainder of his life. His son's body was interred in a mausoleum rather than buried; his mother said that she would never allow his remains to be put into the ground again.[49]

CORPORATE CORRUPTION: THE ENRON/ANDERSEN CASE

Arthur Andersen, a limited partnership formed in 1913, had been the auditor for Enron since 1985 and had seen Enron grow into the seventh largest company in the United States. The relationship between the two organizations had become quite cozy; there was a revolving work pattern that saw employees move casually from jobs in one company to positions in the other.[50] Meanwhile, Andersen endorsed patently fraudulent bookkeeping schemes that Enron executives had concocted. Enron had run up huge debts that it avoided declaring in its annual reports by transferring them to paper partnerships that had been established to hide the company's true financial condition. The partnerships, allegedly as many as 3,000 of them, were defined as independent entities but actually were closely controlled by Enron executives who profited sensationally from such arrangements. Kenneth Lay, Enron's onetime chief executive officer, had divested himself of stock and stock options worth more than $200 million shortly before the company collapsed.[51]

Arthur Andersen was one of the "Big Five" of America's leading accounting firms, with 350 offices in eighty-four countries and 85,000 employees. It was receiving $52 million a year in auditing and consulting fees from Enron, its major client. Ironically, it hired a woman who had taught organizational behavior at the Harvard Business School to lead the company's Ethics and Responsible Business Practices Group, although Andersen itself refused to put into place its own ethics program.[52]

The government essentially had gotten fed up with Arthur Andersen's repetitive wrongdoing. A year before its Enron troubles Arthur Andersen had paid $110 million to settle a class action suit brought by stockholders of Sunbeam. Andersen's auditors also had failed to detect a Ponzi scheme[53] run by the Baptist Foundation of Arizona, and they had settled complaints in that case for $217 million. Then there was a $7 million payout in a suit involving an inflated earnings statement by Waste Management, a conglomerate controlling regional garbage collections, environmental companies, and other businesses. As part of that settlement Andersen had specified that it would not again engage in such behavior.

The end for Arthur Andersen came after a six-week criminal trial, involving ten days of jury deliberation, after which the auditing firm was found guilty of complicity in the Enron lawbreaking. The prosecution had focused its case on the shredding of relevant papers at Andersen offices in Houston, Portland (Oregon), Chicago, and London after managers had learned that the government was suspicious of their auditing of Enron. More than a ton of documents was destroyed as well as some 30,000 e-mails and computer files. A juror noted: "We wanted to find Andersen not guilty and find that they stood up to Enron. But it's clear that [the lawyer] knew investigators were coming and was telling Andersen to abort the evidence."[54] The judge imposed a fine of $500,000 and a sentence of five years probation. Andersen's clients fled to calmer harbors, the company went under, condemned to death by the doctrine of corporate criminal liability, although the more reasonable interpretation might be that Arthur Andersen was not killed but had committed suicide. Stephen Rosoff and his colleagues sum up the events aptly: "The company now acknowledges that it made what it terms 'errors in judgment.' One could respond that wearing a striped tie with a plaid shirt is an 'error in judgment.' What Arthur Andersen did is a *crime*."[55]

The Andersen case challenged the common observation in studies of corporate criminal liability that criminal penalties at best will have only a short-term effect on the guilty business. The argument has been that few customers will stop purchasing toothpaste if the company whose brand they prefer is accused of colluding in an antitrust agreement with competitors. Nor will an occupational safety and health violation impact profit margins of a multinational corporation. During the Vietnam war, the Dow Chemical Company, the manufacturer of Agent Orange and napalm, poisons used against Vietcong soldiers and civilians, was boycotted by protesters in the United States and paid out $180 million to American servicemen to settle their claims against it.[56] But it did not require the lapse of much time before Dow Chemical's role in the wartime tragedies that had aroused so much fury was largely forgotten—and the company prospered.

Arthur Andersen, however, relied not only on the integrity of the work it performed but also on its good name. Nobody truly had to have Andersen's auditing services; the same services were readily available elsewhere. Taint and dishonor drove a huge enterprise into the ground. The first to desert the sinking ship were the overseas branches, which typically arranged to go independent or to merge with other firms. Two years after the collapse of their employer, former Arthur Andersen workers were supporting an Internet website on which they shared job information and commiserated with each other. Only 215 persons, largely attorneys and administrative staff charged with cleanup up things, remained of the firm's 28,000 domestic employees.

But the story did not end there. In mid-2005, a unanimous US Supreme Court agreed with the claim of the company's lawyers that the shredding of papers—the core of the government case—could have been a routine act, part of a "document rotation policy," and not necessarily part of a cover-up. The jury instructions at the Andersen trial, the Supreme Court opinion noted, had failed to convey the requisite consciousness of wrongdoing that needed to be proved to convict. "For example," Chief Justice William Rehnquist declared, "the jury was told that even if the petitioner honestly and sincerely believed its conduct was lawful, it can be convicted."[57] The reversal of the conviction highlighted several basic issues in regard to white-collar offenses. The court's decision could be read as a demonstration of the skill of corporate attorneys to thwart what most people probably would see as a just punishment of Andersen for its wayward behavior. The outcome also can be interpreted as further evidence of the difficulty of successfully prosecuting even egregious corporate white-collar crimes. Others could see the result as testifying to the failure of government lawyers to compete with the private bar that represents indicted businesses. Some realists, for their part, might regard the Supreme Court's ruling as rather meaningless, except perhaps as a warning about future government actions. After all, Andersen was defunct; its empire destroyed. But that situation too poses a dilemma not easily resolved. Was it fair and just to punish the innocents in Arthur Andersen rather than going after the wrongdoers as individual offenders?

THE SARBANES-OXLEY ACT

The demise of Arthur Andersen was probably the most eye-opening consequence in the panoply of corporate scandals that surfaced in the United States soon after the beginning of the new millennium. Previously, such lawbreaking had been shrugged off as an unfortunate but exceedingly rare occurrence. But analysts now insisted that the kinds of scams that marked the affairs of Andersen, Enron, WorldCom, Global Crossing, Adelphia, General Re, the American International Group (AIR), ImClone, and Tyco International were not uncommon but had remained in the dark during periods of financial prosperity. Corporate earnings statements often were wildly inflated, but the manipulations could be camouflaged so long as onlookers were becalmed by a heady rise in the value of their holdings.[58] There was some irony in the situation because executives in competing companies who operated honestly were being downgraded for their failure to show a growth rate equivalent to that of the cheaters. WorldCom's fabrications about its profits and the amount of Internet traffic its network was carrying made competitors such as AT&T and Sprint appear inefficient. In an effort to keep pace with WorldCom's fictitious claims, the honest companies overinvested in new technology and engaged in price wars, layoffs, and in the case of AT&T, a decision to break up the company. [59]

Legislators in the United States commonly react, as we noted earlier, to scandals such as that at Enron and its criminal compeers with new laws that often are more symbolic than satisfactory. They try to close loopholes, almost invariably increase penalties, and hope for the best.

The Sarbanes-Oxley Act (more formally known as the Public Company Reform and Investor Protection Act)[60] is the legislative consequence of the outbreak, or perhaps the discovery, of corporate lawbreaking. It applies to publicly held companies and to certified public accountants, though companies not registered in the United States, a growing roster, remain beyond its reach. The legislation addresses one of the more egregious outrages of the Andersen case by forbidding auditors to engage in non–audit services for a client unless such services are approved by the client's board of directors. It mandates that chief executive officers and chief financial officers attest to the honesty of the company's quarterly profit-and-loss statements. If the certification is false, the chief executive officer and/or the chief financial officer must reimburse the company for any equity-based compensation and any profit from the sale of stock received during the year following the noncompliant audit report. It also prohibits executives and other specified company officers from accepting employment with the company's auditor for at least two years after they have given up their original position. In addition, the statute of limitation for corporate offenses was changed to two years from the time of the discovery of the act or five years from the time of the commission of the alleged crime, thus overturning a Supreme Court decision that had invoked a shorter time period during which an offender could be prosecuted.[61] Lead auditors must be rotated every five years, and an audit cannot be done by a firm for whom the chief executive officer or chief financial officer worked within the past five years. Also, audit documents must be retained for at least five years, and no personal loans can be made by a company to its executives.

The Act created two new felonies. The first punishes any person or company that knowingly alters, destroys, mutilates, conceals, or covers up any document or tangible object with the intent to obstruct or impede procedures of federal agencies or bankruptcy investigators. This represents what is undoubtedly the most severe—and arguably the most controversial—section of the Act. Obstruction of justice is a rather ambiguous action, and it provides prosecutors with what can become a very heavy-handed weapon. John Ashcroft, then the attorney general, stressed the intent of the Department of Justice to employ this power whenever the Department deemed it necessary: "[C]orporations that choose to prolong the damage to the public by refusing to cooperate with investigators should be forewarned—if you obstruct, if you impede—you leave your company vulnerable to public indictment, prosecution, and conviction."[62] The second new felony relates to the willful destruction or secreting of corporate audit records. Punishments are set at a maximum of twenty years for the first-named offense, ten for the second.[63]

That the Sarbanes-Oxley Act is no panacea, although it may be an improvement on current arrangements, was highlighted by developments soon after it was signed into law. The measure called for the appointment of a Public Accounting Oversight Board to establish auditing standards. The first person appointed as chair of the committee was seen as so beholden to corporate interests that he had to resign before he was confirmed in office. When the Board first met, it voted each member an annual salary of $432,000 and its chair more than half a million dollars. These initial moves seemed to many onlookers more in the spirit of the financial piracy that had led to the creation of the Board than in the spirit of commendable public service.

The first case to contest the constitutionality of the law was decided in favor of the government near the end of 2004. Richard M. Scrushy was the founder and chairman and chief executive officer of HealthSouth, the nation's largest rehabilitative hospital corporation. Health South was headquartered in Birmingham, Alabama, with some 50,000 employees worldwide. Scrushy was a local nabob. He earned $267 million from the company between 1996 and 2002, and had a library, a ballpark, and a building named after him. There also was a statute, but after someone painted the word "Thief" on it, the statue was pulled down. Scrushy was indicted for fifty-eight counts of having certified fraudulent accounting reports that involved misstatements in the amount of $2.7 billion. His lawyers claimed that the requirements of the statute were "so vague as to defy comprehension." Judge Karon O. Bowdre said that jurors would have to decide such matters as the reach of the law and whether Scrushy had "willfully" signed the false accounting report.[64] Wags, discussing the case on the television show *60 Minutes* joked that if Scrushy were convicted that it wouldn't be long before he would have the jail named after him.

But Scrushy was not convicted. Again, as was true in the Andersen case, the outcome demonstrated the impressive ability of affluent persons and entities charged with white-collar crimes to triumph in court. In the voir dire examinations before the Scrushy trial, a juror, who later was seated on the panel, had been asked: "Are you going to hold it against Mr. Scrushy that he hired that many lawyers?" The juror's response captures an essential element of white-collar cases. "Certainly not," he said. "That's the way our system works. You hire the best."[65]

Post-mortems on the Scrushy case sought to comprehend why he had been acquitted when Bernard J. Ebbers, the former CEO of WorldCom, and Dennis Kozlowski, the onetime head of Tyco, both had been convicted on evidence no more compelling than that against Scrushy. It was noted that both Ebbers and Kozlowski had taken the witness stand in their own defense and that this had offered prosecutors an opportunity to pinpoint their lies, evasions, and discomfort when confronted with incriminating evidence. Scrushy had declined to testify, a matter that in the United Kingdom may be commented upon by the judge as a possible adverse circumstance, a procedure not permitted in U.S. courts. Also both Ebbers and Kozlowski has been tried in New York City, while Scrushy's case was heard in Birmingham, Alabama, where he was known and respected for his philanthropy. In addition, Scrushy, right before and during his trial, affiliated closely with an African-American church in the city. Six of the original twelve jurors were African-Americans, and that number rose to seven when one white juror was dismissed because of illness.[66]

Pamela H. Bucy, a legal scholar at the University of Alabama who is well known for her work on white-collar crime,[67] thought that the Scrushy verdict reflected the fact that the defendant's highly-paid legal team "out-lawyered" the prosecutors. "If you look at the evidence, it's a surprising verdict," Bucy said. If you look at how the case went in the courtroom, it's not a surprise."[68]

Matters took various other turns after Scrushy's acquittal. He was being sued by stockholders for equity losses they had suffered, and at the same time, he was suing HealthSouth for $70 million, alleging that the company had unfairly terminated him. The SEC scheduled a civil trial against Scrushy for mid-2007, and he was hit with a judgment for $48 million for "unjust enrichment" at the expense of shareholders. On top of this, he was facing a bribery charge on the ground that he had given former Governor John Siegelman a contribution of $500,000 in exchange for a seat on the state board that regulated hospitals. In the midst of all this, Scrushy had founded his own church and had played a prominent role in the formation of the Kingdom Builders International Ministries to provide food for Africans and to perform a range of other services to poor people.

CORPORATE GOVERNANCE

The doctrine of corporate criminal liability has produced a voluminous outpouring of scholarly analyses. An attempt by the current author and a colleague to put together a bibliography of this material located 718 references, most of which have appeared in the last three decades.[69] The current spotlight regarding corporate criminal liability focuses on what is labeled "corporate governance."

Basically, corporate governance guidelines call for sufficient oversight by the board of directors to assure that the business obeys the law and that the interests of customers and shareholders are adequately protected. Warren Buffett has indicated that "the ability and the fidelity of managers have long needed monitoring" and that "accountability and stewardship withered in the last decade" because "too many people in recent years have behaved badly at the office, fudging numbers, and drawing obscene pay for mediocre business achievement."[70] This last observation was reinforced by a survey based on corporate proxy statements that found that the total direct compensation of the highest officer of major American companies—a figure that includes salary, bonuses, gains from options exercised, other long-term incentive payouts, and the value of restricted shares—advanced 16.4 percent from 2002 to 2003 and reached an average annual sum of $3.6 million a person.[71]

Buffett indicated that boards of directors must be more diligent in discovering and firing inept and/or corrupt managers, and he suggested, on the basis of his own lifetime service on the boards of nineteen companies, that the problem often lies in the unwillingness of well-mannered directors to rock the boat by questioning what might be unsavory activities. Buffett suggested that boards meet outside the presence of company executives. At Berkshire-Hathaway, the company Buffett runs, directors are paid but a pittance so that they have little to lose by speaking up when they think something is awry. In addition, and uncommonly, they are not provided with liability insurance. This approach, Buffett said, had saved the company millions of dollars over the years.[72]

The dramatic consequence of the failure of corporate governance is reflected in the results of the 2004 survey of the reputations of American corporations. "Big corporations," the report noted, "are stuck in the doghouse," despite the two years that had gone by since the height of the scandals in the corporate world. Conducted by the Hartt Interactive and the Reputation Institute, of Rochester, New York, the survey found that "the public's scorn runs deeper than the scandals." Company scores had dropped in regard to customer service, environmental policies, and the treatment of employees. A senior vice president of the survey firm noted that "too many companies think they can simply advertise their way out of a bad reputation."[73]

Corporate criminal liability, it appears, reflects that age-old distrust of the power and the temptations that permeate the world of business. A primary reason for the failure of law to be able to control corporate crime satisfactorily may lie in the fact that legal institutions are made to last, whereas business institutions are designed for rapid adaptation to changing economic and technological realities."[74]

Whatever the core explanation, it is clear that the use of the doctrine of corporate criminal liability has captured the attention of Americans, at least temporarily. Our crystal ball becomes a bit murky when we try to peer into the future of the doctrine in the United States. But two matters stand out, working in opposing directions. First, the plethora of corporate scandals that recently have come to light has alerted politicians and their constituents to the possibility of serious corporate wrongdoing. It is arguable whether the wrongdoers are bad apples in an untainted barrel or whether they are part of a large group of malefactors who pervade the corporate world, only a few of whom happen to get caught.

Second, though there was a great flurry of public concern and extensive law enforcement action in the wake of the scandals, the subject of corporate crime lost a good part of its hold on the public imagination in the United States when the country's armed forces invaded Iraq and the uncertainty and horrors of the occupation of that country came to dominate public discussion.

It seems evident that corollary conditions will have a very strong effect on the future of corporate crime control. If there are no overshadowing events, we would predict that there will be a serious and continuing effort to place corporations on a much tighter leash. For one thing, the American public is deeply concerned about the migration overseas—the outsourcing—of jobs. And given the very large fiscal deficit that the country now runs, it is likely that corporations will be taxed much more heavily and criminal penalties imposed to make certain that they pay what they honestly owe.

The Internal Revenue Service (IRS) now requires thirty-eight months to audit corporate tax returns, an important explanation for why the agency was not involved in uncovering any of the notorious scandals. Tax collections from corporations fell to $133 billion in the 2003 fiscal year that ended on September 30, the second lowest total since 1983. In 1970, corporations contributed 17 percent of the nation's budget by their tax payments; today, that figure has dropped to 7 percent. The 1,300 largest corporations are audited rather scrupulously by the government, but the 148,000 other corporations have only a 4 percent chance that their tax return will be scrutinized.[75]

Nobody seriously disputes that the decline in assessments paid by corporations is in some considerable measure the result of fraud that goes undetected, with estimates ranging as high as $20 billion a year being illegally withheld from the government.[76] Besides more efficient, timely, and comprehensive auditing, it is not beyond imagining that criminal enforcement agencies might begin to intrude more directly into corporate affairs, perhaps to the extent of placing undercover agents on the premises of suspected law violators.

Beyond these measures, there probably will come a time when corporations will be required to register in the federal jurisdiction, thereby homogenizing what now are the variegated requirements of the states, some of which compete for business by making particularly indulgent rules for corporate bodies. There also inevitably will be unpredictable developments, but there is no question that corporate criminal liability is a growth industry.

RESEARCH AND CORPORATE CRIME

The relative neglect of research regarding corporate offenses and the focus on individual malefactors has been one of the odder developments in the study of white-collar crime. After a recent review of what has been written on the subject, Sally Simpson noted that corporate crime control is a "complex subject" and that "in spite of many suggestions about how it might be accomplished (many of which are based on ideological preferences), few strategies have been explored empirically or systematically." She was, she writes, "especially surprised by the woeful lack of research on corporate deterrence, especially from a criminological perspective."[77]

The relative inattention to corporate crime occurs despite the fact that that the study of crime to a considerable extent has been the academic territory of persons trained in sociology, a discipline that tends to focus on the role of institutional and organizational considerations in he fashioning of human behavior rather than on individuals who perform the behavior. It has to be granted that what a person does is in considerable measure a function of the experiences that the person has undergone since—and even perhaps before—birth. Psychologists typically concentrate on the person, as he or she is, at the time the behavior ensues. Yet criminologist theory, as we will note in much greater detail in the following chapter, has tended to ignore the formative context of social systems that produce or inhibit crime and to attend to the person; in the leading theoretical postulate today, the emphasis is on an absence of self-control without attending to the social structure that might induce or reinforce such a trait.

Sutherland's original examination of the criminal and regulatory records of corporations in his classic *White Collar Crime* undoubtedly resulted, as research often does, because pertinent material was available and easy to access. Plentiful records of actions taken against corporations can be found in existing archives and court records. It is quite another matter to pinpoint the genesis and characteristics of individual actors in these corporate offenses, even when they are prosecuted alone or, more often, in tandem with the corporate entity.

In the most ambitious and significant inquiry into white-collar crime by Stanley Wheeler and his colleagues at Yale University, information on offenders, including corporate violators, was gleaned from the presentence reports of federal probation officers.[78] Such reports are quite reliable for static information, such as age, education, and marital status, but they become much more iffy when the officer pretends to discover the roots of the behavior by questioning his client. For one thing, sensible persons on the verge of being sentenced will offer what they believe is the most compelling tale of why they did what they did, regardless of its truth, even presuming they know the truth. The Wheeler study did not include corporate offenses.

Sutherland's original work inspired Marshall Clinard and Peter Yeager some three decades later to undertake a follow-up examination of corporate offenses. They looked at 1,553 cases that had been field against the 562 largest business during a two-year period, an average of 2.7 violations for each company. Among their proposals, several of which since have been adopted, were these:

- Increase the fine ceilings, with fines to be assessed according to the nature of the violation and in proportion to the company's annual sales.
- Stiffen criminal penalties for violations of health, safety, and environmental regulations that "recklessly endanger" the public or employees.
- Require mandatory publicity for corporate civil and criminal violations.
- Employ imprisonment more extensively with longer sentences. Community service in place of incarceration should be prohibited by law, except for unusual circumstances.
- Do not allow convicted corporate offenders to be indemnified by their companies.[79]

The absence of significant field research on corporate crime that might shed light on important but unresolved matters is unfortunate, although it should be emphasized that such work can be extraordinarily complicated, time-consuming, and often very expensive. Government funding agencies have not been forthcoming with grants for such work, undoubtedly out of a concern that findings regarding corporate crime might have political repercussions and alienate some of the major sources of campaign contributions.

By far, the most satisfactory method for resolving important questions regarding corporate crime would be to launch a comprehensive inquiry, well-funded and staffed by persons with impeccable research credentials. Their charge would be to carry out a research program that identifies key issues that can be answered with empirical evidence and then to seek that evidence. Such an enterprise would be staffed by scholars and technicians representing diverse disciplines, with an overseeing board of prominent public figures who have no axe to grind or, at least, are willing to yield that weapon if they are persuaded that the public interest so requires.

To advocate such a comprehensive research endeavor is to hope for the very best. Absent such an approach, what kinds of tactics might individual scholars and research teams look at to begin to provide empirical insight into corporate crime?

First, there needs to be a systematic public annual accounting of lawbreaking by corporate entities. Such an endeavor would be daunting; two particularly talented social scientists visited the issue at some length before virtually throwing up their hands at the complexities involved in the task.[80] But it can be done. A law professor, noting the need for such numbers, pointed out that Congress could readily amend the securities law to require corporations to report all criminal indictments and convictions during a specified time period.[81] The result would have flaws, but so do the FBI reports whose strength is that they presumably measure the same thing—even if it is not the whole picture—year after year.[82]

Second, there is a need to carry out fieldwork, primarily of a qualitative nature, on site (that is, inside corporations or as close as one can get to the scene) to obtain an understanding of the dynamics of decisions to violate the law. There is an understandable tendency to avoid this kind of demanding research effort in favor of manipulating readily available data, such as information on corporate size and net income as these correlate with offending. Such studies, as Eugene Szwajkowski observes in advocating them, are "especially attractive because the indicators cited can be readily computed or accessed without gaining access to the firm itself."[83] Well and good, but the elegant mathematical analyses that result usually fail to provide an adequate understanding of the dynamics, the human cognition, that produced the violations. Earnings might have been weak, but there would be both legal and illegal pathways available for trying to address the problem.

Valuable findings on corporate crime could be derived from what sociologists call participant observation.[84] In this approach, an outsider moves inside and seeks to gain the trust of members of the organization. The focus need not be on wrongdoing; it would seem equally important to determine why some entities conform meticulously to the demands of the law. There are obvious ethical questions that would require resolution, including whether the group should be informed that its members are being used (or, perhaps, exploited).

In addition, there are many specific matters that would benefit from research probes. Answers might vary with the precise behavior being considered rather being responsive to an overarching theme that equally seeks to explain insider trading, antitrust violations, environmental crimes, and false advertising. The following chapter will examine this issue more closely.

What follows here is an illustrative list of ten research suggestions to upgrade our understanding of corporate crime:

1. The subject could benefit from more authoritative insight into the ingredients of corporate decision making and the consequences of different forms of such activity. A particularly comprehensive social science study of the processes by which a fatal (but not criminal) corporate policy decision was reached has been offered in Diane Vaughan's *The Challenger Launch Decision*.[85] Vaughan supplies a careful analysis of what led the space launch to end in disaster. Essentially, as she saw it, incremental and well-meaning—perhaps even necessary—compromises, none of which had untoward consequences, underlay the fatal explosion of the space craft. Vaughan's detailed and exquisitely argued conclusions led to an invitation to appear on the nationally televised program *60 Minutes*, but the invitation was withdrawn when the producers learned that Vaughan had located the blame

for the disaster on the intricate and complex pattern of decision making and not on evil people. The program wanted villains, not process analysis.

2. How do juries react to high-level, powerful corporate crime defendants? Are they more reluctant to find them guilty than they are street offenders? Views vary. John Coffee, Jr. maintains that in safety and health cases "the odds are high that these laws will be substantially offset when sentencing judges confront 'flesh and blood' defendants having impeccable backgrounds, community ties, and tearful families."[86] Leo Barille disagrees, saying, undoubtedly correctly, "this is not true of many trials."[87] But we do not know for how many trials the observation is correct and why this is so: is it the nature of the defense, the complexity of the charge, public opinion, the media, or combinations of these considerations and many others?

There is a rich research literature on jury reactions to a variety of situations, including the status of the offender and the offense charged.[88] Studies tend to support the view that higher status offenders, while they might benefit initially because of their prestige, are likely to be treated more severely than ordinary defendants when the violation is egregious.[89] Little is known, however, about corporations as defendants in a criminal jury trial. Research could resolve the different positions adopted by Coffee and Barille as well as a host of other issues regarding the ingredients of trials of corporations and the strengths and weakness of corporate liability as opposed to or in concert with individual liability of corporate employees.

3. We need to learn more about the impact of criminal actions on different levels of employees. Brent Fisse and John Braithwaite, in a groundbreaking field study, interviewed officers whose corporations had been involved in notorious offenses and discovered that they were very disturbed about the reactions of friends and neighbors, reactions that extended even to remarks made to their children by schoolmates.[90] Very likely, different considerations operate in different cases. A research endeavor would have to attend to the consequences of what happens at various points along the criminal justice continuum—the first publicity about the case, the indictment, preliminary hearing or grand jury proceedings, the trial, the verdict, and the sentence.

4. Basic to the debate about corporate crime is the question of whether civil or criminal liability ought to be the preferred prosecutorial path. Questions abound on this issue: If only civil suits could be filed against corporate entities, would prosecutors be more dedicated to locating a guilty individual and proceeding against that person criminally? If so, what consequences might this have for deterrence, justice, and similar matters? Since civil proceeds require a lower standard of proof, will there be more decisions adverse to the corporation than if the criminal route had been taken?

5. An interesting avenue of exploration would involve comparison of foreign jurisdictions that operate without the possibility of corporate criminal penalties. Albert Alschuler offers a testable hypothesis:

> My guess is that the imposition of civil sanctions through less burdensome judicial and administrative procedure in Europe results not only in greater fairness but also in more effective regulation. Our efforts to stigmatize aggregations of people, most of whom are blameless, are unjustified in principle and may be less effective in practice than civil alternative would be.[91]

A particularly good comparison might be that between Japan and the United States. The Japanese penal code has no general provision for corporate criminal responsibility, though it can be imposed as a statutory exception for acts of environmental pollution. Moreover, in Japan a corporate conviction cannot be imposed without proving criminality on the part of an individual representative of the business firm.[92] The paradox here is that Japanese culture tends to emphasize collective responsibility for wrongdoing, while the ethos in the United States is notably individualistic.[93] Russia (and the Soviet Union before) never adopted corporate criminal liability because the doctrine is said not to be "compatible with the tradition of our legal system."[94] It could make a profitable site for comparison with the United States.

Such research assuredly is fraught with difficulties inherent in the diverse legal, social, and economic nature of the cultures and often involves complications introduced by language differences, but the challenge of the work, and its likely yield, makes it a high-priority research item.

6. Kenneth Dau-Schmidt has argued that corporate wrongdoing is criminalized only because the society does not regard it seriously enough.[95] Were people to consider corporate crime to be especially blameworthy, he maintains, they would attack these acts more efficiently by suing the companies under tort law. This is at best an arguable position. The sociologist Donald Black maintains precisely the opposite: "In modern societies, groups, especially business organizations, are often sued for compensatory damages. If fact, this seems to be all that people normally want from the organizations that have victimized them."[96] Such contradictory positions cry out for empirical resolution. Research might begin to gather information on why, if they do not, victims of corporate crime fail to take their grievance to the civil courts, and whether such decisions are influenced by the prospect of criminal actions. What happens in the United States most certainly must be influenced by the practice of contingency fees (not allowed in Britain) in which attorneys keep for themselves something in the vicinity of one-third of a tort award. Few lawyers will gamble against heavy odds and most undoubtedly calculate carefully how much they are likely to receive from a jury (subject to the judge's possible subsequent adjustment) and how much time and energy the endeavor is likely to cost them.

7. "Where penalties are high individuals will fight while firms will settle," John Coffee says.[97] What are the precise details of this process? How "high" must the penalties be—and how are financial impositions and/or the possibility of imprisonment to be calibrated? Is a corporate criminal fine of half a million dollars seen as "higher" than, say, a civil fine of three quarters of a million dollars? That is, what force does a criminal ruling add to a civil penalty?

8. John Coffee also puts forward another proposition whose empirical resolution would contribute significantly to the debate on corporate crime. "Corporate liability," he states, "may make it easier to convict the individual defendants. In any multidefendant prosecution, the interests of the defendants are at least potentially adverse, since each can generally gain concessions by implicating others. The corporation is no exception to this rule and is in a position to provide evidence against individual defendants or to discipline them, in return for leniency for itself."[98] How often and under what

circumstances does this scenario come into play? And how often does the opposite occur, that defendants become witnesses against the corporation in exchange for leniency for themselves? And how does this square with Coffee's observation that "law enforcement officials cannot afford to ignore either the individual or the firm in choosing their targets, but they can realize important economies of scale by simultaneously pursuing both."[99] Such a sweeping judgment may do injustice to the very considerable variety of results that evolve from pursuing the corporation alone, individuals only, or both. What in fact are these things?

There also is another element in these complex interactions. It is believed that juries at times compromise, acquitting individual defendants and convicting the corporation in order to avoid putting a criminal label upon a white-collar defendant. But as one writer observes: "There appears to be little empirical support bearing upon this assumption and so commentators have cited each other for support."[100]

9. Research attention could profitably be directed toward the practice of indemnification by the corporation of its officers for their legal expenses when they are charged criminally for actions that were done as part of their employment. It is claimed that in jurisdictions where such a practice is allowed it undermines the possible deterrent effect of the prosecutory action.[101] It can be argued that an awareness of the financial protective shield might encourage employees to undertake actions that they otherwise would avoid if they knew that the full cost of their prosecution and penalty would fall upon them rather than on the corporation. On the other hand, frivolous or unwarranted charges against corporate officers, which they have to defend out of their own pocket, could put corporate personnel in an unfair situation. Besides which, it could inhibit arguably legal ventures that would advance the company's well-being. This is a subject about which we could use a good deal of solid information.

10. "It would be reasonable," Leonard Orland has written, "to hypothesize that executive criminals are treated far less harshly when their corporation is *party* to the crime than when the corporation is the *victim* of the crime."[102] Is this true?

SUMMING UP

Orland has criticized what he believes is the ill-advised manner in which social scientists who lack training in law venture into the study of white-collar and corporate crime. He observes that "despite the extraordinary expansion of the legal concept of corporate crime, both by Congress and the federal courts, the study of corporate crime remains a curiously neglected area of scholarship. The legal literature is astonishingly thin, and the nonlegal literature is hopelessly misguided."[103] In terms of sheer volume, matters have improved considerably since Orland made these observations more than two decades ago. What continues to be missing is not the degree of attention devoted to the subject but the scientific sophistication of the information and insights regarding it.

The development of the doctrine of corporate criminal liability was the result almost exclusively of expediency rather than of empirical evidence. This is not to say that what came about is necessarily wrong, only that is has not received the research attention that could resolve many nagging and very important issues. Put another way, what now exists in law and practice could be wrong in terms of what it seeks to achieve. David Riesman, an eminent practitioner of social science who also held a law degree, once noted that lawyers are "very apt to be scornful of the findings of social science."[104] Supreme Court Justice Louis Brandeis, however, endorsed the idea that "a lawyer who has not studied economics and sociology is very apt to become a public enemy."[105] That rhetoric may be overblown, but it can be supplemented by the more muted observation of Supreme Court Justice Felix Frankfurter: "The problems that are the respective preoccupations of anthropology, economics, law, psychology, sociology, and related areas of scholarship," Frankfurter wrote, "are merely departmentalized dealings, by way of manageable division of analysis, with interpenetrating perplexities."[106]

It remains necessary, in these terms, to heed the warning of a British parliamentary report that emphasized the importance of carefully evaluating public policies: "It is both wasteful and irresponsible to set experiments in motion and omit to record and analyze what happens," the report observed. "It makes no sense in terms of administrative efficiency and, however little intended, it indicates a cavalier attitude toward human welfare."[107]

[4]

DEFINITIONS AND THEORIES

"Love and marriage, love and marriage," the 1955 lyrics written by Jimmy Van Heusen and Sammy Cahn proclaimed, "They go together like a horse and carriage." The song, which soared to the heights of popularity when rendered by Frank Sinatra, further declared: "This I tell you, brother. You can't have one without the other."

It is an enchanting melody with captivating lyrics, but the statement being made is far from accurate. There is a great deal of love without marriage and much marriage without love. I quote the lyrics to start the present chapter because we find similar kinds of disconnects between definitions of white-collar crime and theories that attempt to explain it. There are definitions that call into question particular theories; and there are theories that fail to shed satisfactory light on what is defined as white-collar crime. There is an occasional apparent beneficent marriage between theory and definition, but most such liaisons limp along on a rocky road and, to retain the ice cream image momentarily, end up as banana splits. Perhaps love and marriage are best understood as separate phenomena. It is also arguable whether it is possible to comprehend white-collar crime theoretically as a unitary phenomenon, or whether it makes more sense to establish homogeneous forms of such lawbreaking and/or its perpetrators when the aim is to understand in theoretical terms what goes on.

How subjects such as white-collar and corporate crime are defined and the theories that are employed to explain them are likely to have a strong impact on the kind of research that is conducted and the power of the conclusions that are reached. If white-collar crime is declared to embrace shoplifting by college students, theoretical explanations will differ from those based on a definition that includes only frauds by chief financial officers that exceed $1 million in illegal gain. It therefore is essential to determine what kinds of definitions have been offered concerning white-collar crime before examining the explanatory theories that have been put forward.

DEFINING WHITE-COLLAR CRIME

Few, if any, criminological terms are surrounded by as much dispute as white-collar crime. We briefly noted in the initial chapter that Edwin H. Sutherland, the progenitor of the concept of white-collar crime, offered a number of relatively complementary but rather imprecise definitions of his subject matter. One explanation for Sutherland's failure to formulate a scientifically satisfactory and indisputable characterization of white-collar crime, we noted, might have been the fact that his theory, which he labeled "differential association," was put forward as the key to understanding all crime; therefore, there was no need to differentiate one type from another, at least for the purpose of generating theoretical axioms. Burglary, rape, fraud, and the extensive list of other delicts were for Sutherland a consequence of learning. To understand any of them involved determining what a person had learned from others about these acts and what attitudes regarding their commission had been absorbed by the offender.

Sutherland had accepted the premise of a colleague and research collaborator, Thorsten Sellin, who maintained that statutes failed to provide a satisfactory basis for social science studies of criminal behavior because laws often are fortuitous consequences of the powers and the whims of those who create them and do not arise intrinsically from the nature of the subject matter. Put simply, Sellin was saying that many social harms go unattended and many insignificant acts are outlawed, and that it is the obligation of social scientists to create categories aside from the law that allow them to examine behaviors that are equivalent in their consequences rather than those which, sometimes by chance, become embedded in penal codes.[1] This view has received some support over the years. Laureen Snider, a highly regarded Canadian scholar, for instance, has written that "upperworld criminals and corporations . . . have been successful in defining their own acquisitive acts as noncriminal and even harmless, despite the reams of data that have documented the heavy dollar losses and even heavier loss of life and limb they cause." She concludes: "Although the legal political authorities may not be legally able to criminalize such acts, that does not mean that we, as anlaysts, cannot."[2]

Definitions of white-collar crime that have been advanced sometimes attend to Sellin's views, though more recently they are likely to ignore or to reject them. What follows is an inventory of the best-known definitions of white-collar crime.

Edwin H. Sutherland (1939a)

In his 1939 presidential address to the American Sociological Society, Sutherland did not linger long on the matter of definition. His focus, he said, was on "crime in the upper or white-collar class, composed of respectable or at least respected business and professional men."[3]

The phrase "or at least respected" has a slight touch of the sarcastic and the omission in the definition of politicians was not in keeping with the details that Sutherland would offer of white-collar crimes. He entered a disclaimer by adding that his concern was with "the purpose of developing the theories of criminal behavior, not for the purpose of muckraking or of reforming anything except criminology."[4] Nobody listening to what Sutherland said and to what he later wrote on the subject could have taken this comment seriously. It was obvious that his presentation was fueled by a distaste, often rising to the level of outrage, regarding white-collar crime.

Perhaps uneasy about his terse definitional sidebar, Sutherland in the published version of his address added a footnote that can be said only to have created more confusion than enlightenment. It read:

> Perhaps it should be repeated that "white-collar" (upper) and "lower" classes merely designate persons of high and low socioeconomic status. Income and the amount of money involved in the crime are not the sole criteria. Many persons of "low" socioeconomic status are white-collar criminals in the sense that they are well-dressed, well-educated and have high incomes, but "white-collar" as used in this paper means "respected," "socially accepted and approved," "looked up to." Some people in this class may not be well dressed or well

educated, nor have high incomes, although the "upper" classes usually exceed the "lower" classes in these respects, as well as in social status.[5]

As an exegetic exercise, this paragraph would seem to challenge the mightiest minds to make definitive sense of it. What seems to be the clearest pronouncement may also be the most confusing: the statement that persons of low socioeconomic status can be white-collar criminals since they sometimes are well-dressed, well-educated, and have high incomes. To have a high income would by most standards not be equivalent to low socioeconomic status, particularly if the person is also well educated. Then there is the fudge word "but" to introduce the sentence that reiterates that Sutherland is concerned with persons who are "respected" and "socially accepted and approved." Finally, we have the observation of the obvious, that the upper classes usually do better financially and in terms of education than the lower classes.

Something seems to have been bothering Sutherland. Perhaps he was concerned with others misidentifying some group of offenders as white-collar criminals that he did not desire to have put into the category, although it is not obvious what exactly he had in mind. Deservedly, Sutherland's footnote stab at definitional clarity largely has been ignored by later commentators on white-collar crime.

Sutherland followed his brief attention to definitions with the declaration that criminal statistics showed that "less than two percent of the persons committed to prisons in a year belong to the upper class."[6] One wonders where this number, offered without a cite, was derived from because, if we knew, it would help us to arrive at a clearer understanding of what Sutherland had in mind in regard to his study population.

The body of Sutherland's address, in which he set out instances of white-collar crime, offered a short roster of magnates from past times: Cornelius Vanderbilt, J. P. Morgan, and A.B. Stickney. As examples from his own time, Sutherland rattled off a list of notorious swindlers, including Ivar Kreuger, Sasha Stavisky, Richard Whitney, Wilbur Foshay, Philip Musica/F. Donald Coster, Albert Fall, and Harry Sinclair. He observed that these were but a segment of "the many other merchant princes and captains of finance and industry and a host of lesser followers" who had engaged in criminal acts.[7]

Sutherland's list of white-collar criminals hardly constitutes a homogeneous group. Take, for example, the first four persons. Swedish-born Ivar Kreuger (1880–1932) had cornered a huge portion of the world's production of matches and in the process accumulated a massive fortune. In 1913, he established Aktiebolaget Sveriges Förande Tändstickfabriker (the Swedish Match Company), which began as a small family-owned operation and grew into a global enterprise with branches in thirty-six countries. Kreuger loaned millions of dollars to financially strapped countries, often in exchange for monopoly privileges in the domestic production of matches. His company paid stunning annual dividend rates of between 16 and 20 percent. But the money was coming not from profits but largely from capital. He ultimately overextended himself and began to employ crooked accounting practices, hiding his losses in the more than 400 subsidiaries that his trust controlled. Kreuger himself was the only person aware of the details of the empire he had created. In one instance, he negotiated financing from several New York banks, using some of his company's stock as collateral. But he arranged the loans so that he could substitute other securities for his original pledge. After Kreuger's death, the holdings he had subsequently deposited with the New York banks were found to be Yugoslavian bonds hardly worth the paper on which they were printed. Similarly, Italian banknotes with a face value of $150 million were found in his vault. When they were presented for redemption to Benito Mussolini, the Italian dictator, he called in his finance minister whose signature was on the bonds. The minister pointed out that the forgery was self-evident: his name had been spelled in three different ways on the notes.

Kreuger was found dead on March 12, 1932, in his Paris apartment across from the Grand Palais. He had left a note in his New York Park Avenue penthouse that read: "I'm too tired to continue." His body was cremated almost immediately and his diaries burned. There were some who insisted that he had been murdered. A writer today, examining the regulation of the New York Stock Exchange, says that the answer to an important question requires but two words. The question is: "Why did the Exchange initiate stringent oversight rules?" The answer is: "Ivan Kreuger."[8]

Kreuger would seem to fit handily within the boundaries of white-collar crime that Sutherland established in his address to the American Sociological Society, but there has to be serious reservations about Sasha (later altered to Serge Alexandre) Stavisky (1886–1934), a swindler who was involved in a series of nefarious maneuvers about the same time as Kreuger was at work. Stavisky and his grandfather first operated on the margins of the world of theaters, nightclubs, and gambling, running various schemes that earned Stavisky two brief jail terms. Once free, he formed a company that claimed to produce soups but, in fact, produced nothing more than advertisements for a nonexistent product. When that effort collapsed, he began to deal in fraudulent stock transactions and counterfeit treasury bonds, which led to his detention in prison for seventeen months while his case was under investigation.

Stavisky finally was released on medical grounds after his trial had been postponed nineteen times. He then began to enlist impressive political and financial figures to serve on the boards of directors of the entities that he established. One company sold Phébor, a wooden refrigerator that was said to require no electricity. It was claimed that it was ideal for the North African market. Unfortunately, however, it did not refrigerate. There also was a land development company that issued shares but owned no land.

Stavisky's greatest coup came in transactions with the *crédits municipaux*—French municipal pawnshops—which he persuaded to issue bonds for the largely fake emeralds that he brought to them. The bonds then were turned into cash or invested in insurance or other legitimate enterprises. When the police in one city caught on to the scheme, Stavisky was able to redeem the jewels with money he had gotten from a similar operation in another part of France. In time, the bonds became due and Stavisky had no resources to pay that debt. He took flight to his chalet in Chamonix, and there killed himself, with the police literally at his doorstep. As in the case of Kreuger, suspicions arose, seemingly unfounded, that he had been murdered in order to keep him from informing on powerful political figures involved in his intrigues.[9]

Stavisky is at best only arguably a person either respectable or respected: he was a conman who never contemplated engaging in an honest enterprise. In this regard, he can be said to remain outside of the parameters that Sutherland set up for his examination of white-collar crime. The same can be said of another entry on Sutherland's list, Musica-Coster. F. Donald Coster (1884–1938) was the name adopted by Brooklyn-born Philip Musica, a dedicated crook who had served prison terms in Canada for bribing a customs office and for forging invoices. He changed his name to Coster, and, although a high school dropout, claimed an MD and Ph.D. from the University of Heidelberg in Germany. He gained control of the McKesson-Robbins, a leading drug company, and proceeded to milk it virtually dry—a haul of $18 million—by a stratagem that involved listing assets allegedly held by nonexistent subsidiaries. Coster, aided by three of his brothers, also using assumed names, and two brothers-in-law carried out his plan for twelve years before being found out. He shot himself in the head when his deception was uncovered. The last paragraph of his four-page suicide note read: "As God is my judge, I am the victim of Wall Street plunder and blackmail in a struggle for honest existence. . . . Oh, merciful God, bring the truth to light."[10] Such self-righteousness often seems to be a hallmark of the mental processes of white-collar criminals.

Stavisky and Musia-Coster, in terms of the financial Potemkin villages they constructed, most reasonably could be classified as "collective embezzlers," the term coined by Kitty Calavita and Henry Pontell to characterize persons who used the savings and loan banks that they gained control of to illegally enrich themselves and who never had any other goal in mind.[11]

Other figures on Sutherland's roster are also something of a mixed bag. Wilbur Burton Foshay (1881–1957), for instance, is a seemingly good fit with Sutherland's understanding of white-collar crime. He is best known for building the Foshay Tower in Minneapolis in 1929, then the tallest building in the Midwest. When the economic depression hit the United States soon after the building was constructed, it was learned that Foshay had been paying dividends on the stock of his gas and oil companies with money received from the latest purchasers—a commonplace pyramid scheme. Foshay's first trial ended in a hung jury, but a woman juror who voted for acquittal was found to have perjured herself by not disclosing to the court that she had worked for ten days with Foshay's colleague, who was on trial with him. She was convicted of perjury and killed herself and her family before the second trial in which Foshay was sentenced to a ten-year prison term. His sentence was commuted to three years by President Franklin Roosevelt and he was later pardoned by President Harry S. Truman. A clue to the attitude underlying Foshay's behavior might lie in the motto he had on his desk: "Why worry? It won't last. Nothing does."[12]

Richard Whitney (1888–1974), who embezzled millions of dollars from trust funds under his care, was a true elite who for some time was president of the New York Stock Exchange. He owned opulent estates, bred horses, and was treasurer of the New York Yacht Club.[13] Albert Fall (1861–1944) and Harry Sinclair (1876–1956) were involved in the 1922 Teaport Dome Scandal. Government oil land near Casper, Wyoming, was leased to Sinclair by Fall, the secretary of the interior in Warren Harding's cabinet, without the required submission of competitive bids. Fall got a one-year prison term while Sinclair was acquitted on the Teapot Dome charge, but he subsequently received a prison sentence for contempt of Congress and for hiring detectives to shadow jury members.[14]

Sutherland also mentions an extensive number of corporate crimes in the list of white-collar offenses, noting investigations of railways, insurance companies, munitions manufacturers, banks, public utilities, stock exchanges, the oil industry, and real estate operations. But his attention was almost exclusively focused on the wrongdoing of individuals who worked in these enterprises. Ten years later, when he published *White Collar Crime*, the emphasis would have shifted almost totally from people to organizations.

Edwin H. Sutherland (1939b)

Sutherland's statement about white-collar crime in the third edition of his textbook seems best viewed as an off-the-cuff formulation that he would back away from by the time he gave the talk. He starts off by pointing out that there is a great deal more crime than the official statistics indicate and that entirely incorrect impressions of crime are formed if conclusions are limited to such statistics. He obviously has in mind white-collar offenses when he notes that some criminals cleverly obey the letter of the law while violating its spirit. Then he goes a step further and observes that some people use bribery and other methods to prevent the enactment of laws to prohibit wrongful and injurious practices:

> The danger from robbery or kidnaping is clearly realized, for they involve direct sensory processes and are based on social relations which have existed for many centuries. Theft by fraudulent advertisements and prospectuses is a recent development, and affects persons who may be thousands of miles away from

the thief. Codes of behavior have not been developed in regard to this behavior. The white-collar criminaloids, however, are by far the most dangerous to society of any type of criminal from the point of view of effects on private property and social institutions.[15]

Sutherland then sets out a five-page roster of forms of white-collar crime, including fraudulent balance sheets prepared by public accountants, misleading advertising, the marketing of securities known to be on the downswing, labeling that misstates the place where products were manufactured, insurance fraud, and bribery. Then there is the hyperbolic claim that "the profession of law would almost disappear if all lawyers who practice fraud and misrepresentation by misstatement and by concealment of the whole truth were disbarred."[16]

These observations remained in the 1955 revised edition that Donald R. Cressey prepared after Sutherland's death.[17] In the sixth edition, published in 1960, the earlier statement that "fraud is unusually prevalent in the legal profession, though official statistics are not available as proof" had been tamed to "fraud is also present in the legal profession."[18]

Edwin H. Sutherland (1945)

In what appears as a prescient anticipation of the critiques that would question the kinds of behaviors that he included as white-collar crimes, Sutherland addressed the issue head-on in 1945 with a paper titled: "Is 'White-Collar Crime' Crime?" Obviously, no one was quarreling with acts that were adjudicated by the courts as criminal offenses. It was those acts handled by civil courts and regulatory agencies that were of concern. Sutherland maintained that fines and punitive damages, although leveled by courts without criminal jurisdiction, were punishments and therefore equivalent to crime. So also were stipulations, injunctions, and cease-and-desist orders, although he granted that the necessary standard of proof for such actions was less than that for criminal convictions and that there was no initial assumption of innocence unless proven guilty beyond a reasonable doubt. His defense here was that many other crimes—for instance, statutory rape, bigamy, and defrauding a hotel keeper—dispense with these presumptions. Then he turned argumentative, insisting that the criminality of many of the acts that he labeled crimes had "not been made obvious by the conventional procedures of criminal law, but was blurred and concealed by special procedures."[19] Sutherland sought to buttress his claim of discriminatory lawmaking and law enforcement by citing the notorious record in regard to the Sherman Antitrust Act of 1890, which was designed to rein in business marauders. Of the criminal actions between 1890 and 1929 in which the government prevailed, 27 percent were against businesses and 71 percent against trade unions.[20] As Kurt Eichenwald has noted about what happened following the passage of the Sherman Act: "The sense of victory was short-lived; the law quickly became derided for its insignificance. Its language was vague, its enforcement spotty. It was riddled with so many loopholes that it was commonly mocked as the 'Swiss Cheese Act.'"[21] Finally, Sutherland maintained that white-collar crime was similar to juvenile delinquency, since "[i]n both cases, the procedures of the criminal law are modified so that the stigma of crime will not attach to the offenders."[22] Sutherland would have been pleased when, many years later, two researchers found that the differences between cases handled civilly and those tried before criminal courts were far fewer than most persons presumed.[23]

Edwin H. Sutherland (1948)

Sutherland further muddied the definitional waters in which the concept of white-collar crime was afloat in a talk that he gave to sociology students and faculty at DePauw University in Greencastle, Indiana, during the spring of 1948. His address was titled "Crimes of Corporations" rather than "White Collar Crime," the latter the title of the monograph that would come out the following year and which was likely either near completion or already being prepared for publication. Sutherland presumably had come to appreciate that concentrating on instances of individual white-collar crime would result in a collection of war stories involving tales of particular illegal exploits that would be exceedingly difficult to use to form the basis for generalizations; there would be so much variation in the way that notorious white-collar criminals carried out their schemes that cumulative causal insights would seem beyond demonstration.

Sutherland had discovered that an inventory of corporate wrongdoing, at least that which had been detected, could be extracted from the files of regulatory agencies and that reasonable attempts could be made, as Sutherland did, to construct corporate rap sheets, albeit at the expense of the logic of tabulating offenses of entities of very different sizes and comparing the result to the illegalities of street offenders. In addition, Sutherland's muckraking instincts, never far from the surface, were best served by putting before the public stories of shameful practices by companies whose names and products were familiar to most Americans but whose wrongful behavior was largely buried in agency files. Nonetheless, despite the shift in focus, Sutherland continued to employ an individual rather than an entity definition in his DePauw University presentation:

> I have used the term white-collar criminal to refer to a person in the upper socioeconomic class who violates the laws designed to regulate his occupation. The term white-collar is used in the sense in which it was used by President Sloan of General Motors, who wrote a book titled *The Autobiography of a White Collar Worker*. The term is used more generally to refer to the wage-earning class which wears good clothes at work, such as clerks in stores.[24]

The fact that Sutherland, usually meticulous in such matters, wrongly cites the Sloan book (it was *Adventures of a White Collar Man*[25]) and that Sloan's book offers absolutely no further enlightenment about what might be the nature of white-collar crime adds to the confusion. A biographical sketch of Sloan, however, notes that he characteristically worse collars "of an arresting height, and as stiff as a Buick mudguard."[26] Perhaps it was this image that had caught in Sutherland's mind.

The earlier part of the DePauw definition remained intact in Sutherland's monograph published the following year, but the final sentence in the quoted paragraph about the wage-earning class and its attire was cut. This would seem to indicate that Sutherland had second thoughts and that he desired to confine his focus to upper-class offenders.

Edwin H. Sutherland (1949a)

In *White Collar Crime*, published ten years after his presidential address, Sutherland offered a great deal more illustrative material but did little to clarify or pin down what he intended by the category of white-collar crime. Again, he buried his major attempt at a definition in a footnote, testifying to his relative indifference to the issue. The footnote included the observation that "'white collar' is used here to refer principally to business managers and executives."[27] The use of the fudge words "approximately" and "principally" is disconcerting, particularly when within two pages of his definition Sutherland illustrated white-collar crime with examples of thefts by employees in chain stores and overcharges by mechanics and watch repairers. In the text he slightly paraphrased his Philadelphia statement by noting that a white-collar crime "may be defined approximately as a crime committed by a person of respectability and high social status in the course of his occupation,"[28] and he added that the definition was meant to exclude "many crimes of the upper class, such as most of their cases of murder, adultery, and intoxication, since these are customarily not part of their occupational procedures."[29] Yet the book primarily considers crimes by corporate entities. In the 1983 edition of *White Collar Crime*, which reinstated material that had been excised from the initial manuscript for fear of lawsuits, an entire chapter is devoted to decisions against the American Smelting and Refining Company, the US Rubber Company, and the Pittsburgh Coal Company.[30]

Donald Cressey, Sutherland's acolyte, and a notably sophisticated scholar in his own right, would sternly scold Sutherland for what Cressey regarded as Sutherland's deviation from concern with human behavior and his focus on organizational lawbreaking. "There is a great difference," Cressey observed, "between what Sutherland said and what he did." What he did, it was pointed out, was to "unthinkingly" attribute human capabilities to corporations. Cressey thought that the focus on corporations was not only unthinking but also "ironic" and "incredible" and that Sutherland "assault[ed] his own common sense by assuming that as corporations commit crimes they do so without acting through their officers, directors, employees, or agents." Cressey quotes Sutherland's observation that "when one firm devises (an illegal method) of increasing profits, other firms become aware of this and adopt it." But, writes Cressey, Sutherland never asked the significant theoretical question "By what process does a firm 'become aware of' and 'adopt' illegal processes? Had he done so," Cressey observed, "he would have been reminded that humans behave but entities do not."[31]

I suspect that Sutherland avoided the intellectual problem that Cressey later would raise by simply ignoring it and hoping that others would do likewise. His dilemma, as I see it, was that he would trivialize his theme if he presented a collection of tales featuring activities of well-placed individual white-collar offenders. He could do so effectively in his short presidential address but could not sustain such an approach in a book-length scholarly monograph. He therefore accumulated available data from federal agencies and court cases and wove this material into a sustainable narrative. But he could not do justice to his theoretical claims, since differential association deals with human behavior and, as Cressey declares, corporations may be deemed criminals under the law, but they are not, except in terms of an anthropomorphic legal fiction, "persons."

Edwin H. Sutherland (1949b)

The most straightforward definition that Sutherland offered has largely gone unattended. It appeared during the same year as the publication of *White Collar Crime*. He reiterated his now-familiar declaration that "the white-collar criminal is defined as a person with high socioeconomic status who violates the laws designed to regulate his occupational activities."[32] Such laws, Sutherland went on to say, can be found in the penal code. Thereafter, he observed:

> The white collar criminal should be differentiated, on the one hand, from the person of lower socioeconomic status who violates the regular penal code or the special trade regulations which apply to him and, on the other hand, from the person of high socioeconomic status who violates the regular penal code in ways not connected with his occupation.[33]

This is as close as Sutherland ever came to specifying an exclusive focus on persons of high economic status, but even here there is uncertainty. While he omits from consideration the person of lower socioeconomic status who violates trade regulations that apply to him, he fails to address a vital point: what about regulations that apply both to persons in the upper and in the lower socioeconomic sectors?

That this question is not unrelated to actual circumstances was illustrated in a 1980, 6-3 decision by the US Supreme Court in the insider trading case of *Chiarella v. United States*. Vincent Chiarella was a markup man for Pendrick Press, a financial printer. Among the materials that he was responsible for formatting was the paperwork on proposed mergers and hostile corporate takeover bids. Until the very last moment, the names of the involved entities were either represented by blank spaces or fictitious names. But Chiarella was able to figure out the actual parties, and in five cases purchased stock that, when the deals came through, brought him slightly more than $30,000 in profit over a period of fourteen months. The Securities and Exchange Commission charged Chiarella with insider trading, and he was sentenced to forfeit his profits and serve a one-year prison term. The US Supreme Court, however, reversed the conviction on the grounds that Chiarella was not a corporate insider and therefore was not obliged to restrain from using confidential information without publicly disclosing the information; therefore, he had not breached a specific fiduciary duty.[34]

Chiarella, of course, is, by court edict, not a criminal at all, but Sutherland obviously was willing to ignore court conclusions if they flew in the face of what he regarded as unassailable evidence of criminality. Presumably, though, he would have been pleased with the court's implicit adoption in this particular case of his idea that to qualify as a white-collar crime an act required the abuse of a powerful position inside the elite structure or, as the court saw the matter, the breach of a specified legal obligation.

It is an uncertain interpretative exercise to comb through his various proclamations to try to determine what Sutherland "truly" meant as the definition of the subject that he had so effectively called to academic and public attention. Certainly, his proposed definitions are uncrystallized and, at times, contradictory. What appears to stand out is the sense that Sutherland was most concerned with the illegal abuse of power by upper-echelon businessmen in the course of their working careers, by high-ranking politicians in regard to bribery and similar criminal acts, and by professionals against the interests of the government and their clients and patients. It is reported that Sutherland once was asked by sociologist Edwin Lemert whether by "white-collar crime" he meant a type of crime committed by a special class of people. He is said to have replied that he "was not sure."[35] Given its progenitor's alleged uncertainty, it is not surprising that someone who tries to perform as a glossarist on the Sutherland texts often is befuddled. Sutherland left a wide open field for those who later—though it took many decades—would seek to override his take on white-collar crime.

The reason for the long shelf life of Sutherland's approach to white-collar crime lies in part in its muckraking and ideological appeal. There is widespread belief among the public that the law and the criminal justice system are riddled with biases that deliberately overlook nefarious acts of the elite and the harm that they create. C. Wright Mills, perhaps the sociologist who earned the greatest public recognition in recent times, put the matter this way: "As news of higher immoralities breaks," Mills wrote, "people often say, 'Well, another one got caught today,' thereby implying the cases disclosed are not odd events involving occasional characters but symptoms of widespread conditions."[36]

Until many decades later, Sutherland's rather haphazard definition reigned supreme, with commentators and researchers using whatever aspect of it suited their fancy and their data. Two important endorsements of Sutherland's general position indicate this situation. In 1980 in the course of an extensive inquiry into the prospects for the government's regularly gathering statistics on white-collar crime (they thought the prospects dim and the task extraordinarily complex) Albert Reiss and Albert Biderman proposed a tighter definition of white-collar offenses than Sutherland had offered but one in the same ballpark:

> White-collar violations are those violations of law to which penalties are attached that involve the use of a violator's position of significant power, influence, or trust in the legitimate economic or political institutional order for the purpose of illegal gain, or to commit an illegal act for personal or organizational gain.[37]

Careful readers will note the deliberate omission of the word "crime" from the definition and those readers taking exception to the definition might balk at the uncertain word "significant" and, perhaps, the omission of violations by persons in the professions.

Five years after the Reiss-Biderman formulation, Sutherland's approach to white-collar crime received a strong endorsement from John Braithwaite, one of the leading scholars in the field, in the course of a thoroughgoing examination of the state of the knowledge on the subject. Braithwaite concluded that "probably the most sensible way to proceed . . . is to stick with Sutherland's definition." This, Braithwaite points out, at least excludes welfare cheating and credit card frauds from the territory.

Thereafter, Braithwaite would "partition the domain into major types of white-collar crime in order to generate sound theory."[38]

THE BACKLASH
Frank Hartung/Ernest Burgess (1950)

A peculiar early squabble over the Sutherland definition of white-collar crime arose in connection with the publication of the results of Frank Hartung's study of violators of wartime meat-rationing regulations. Hartung's focus was not on whether these malefactors could be considered white-collar criminals—he assumed they could, at least in terms of the definition he employed: "A white-collar offense is defined as a violation of law regulating business, which is committed for a firm by the firm or its agents in the conduct of its business."[39] What particularly marked Hartung's contribution, however, was the feisty response it drew from Ernest W. Burgess, a preeminent member of the sociology faculty at the University of Chicago. Burgess insisted that persons violating regulatory laws, such as black marketers, could not reasonably be regarded as criminals because they did not so view themselves and were not so viewed by the public. Besides, Burgess maintained, this would mean that half the country's population, given the widespread disregard of wartime rationing, were criminals, a conclusion that Burgess found intellectually intolerable.[40] Hartung attempted to assuage Burgess, a power in the discipline, but he had understandable difficulty with the idea that a person is not a criminal unless that person and the public so regard him or her. It did not seem sensible, for instance, that an antitrust price-fixer who thought himself blameless—he was only trying to protect employees' jobs—and so convinced the public (it is unclear whether Burgess means all of the public, a majority of it, or some part of it) should be differentiated from a person who committed a similar crime and felt guilty about it, whether or not public opinion believed he should.

Paul W. Tappan (1947)

It is from legal scholars that Sutherland has taken the most heat. Paul Tappan, the first of the critics, held a sociology degree from the University of Wisconsin and law degrees from New York University and Columbia

University. He was a discussant of the paper by Hartung, mentioned earlier, that was presented during the 1956 meetings of the American Sociological Society, and that so aroused Ernest Burgess's ire. Subsequently, Tappan wrote an article, "Who Is the Criminal?" that he submitted to the *American Journal of Sociology*. The article cuts to the core of the uncertain nature of what was being called "white-collar crime." "One seeks in vain for criteria to determine this white-collar criminality," Tappan insisted. "It is the conduct of one who wears a white collar and who indulges in occupational behavior to which some particular criminologist takes exception. It may easily be a term of propaganda. For purposes of empirical research or objective description, what is it?"[41]

Tappan offers the following further observation:

> We seek a definition of the white-collar criminal and find an amazing diversity, even among those flowing from the same pen, and observe that characteristically they are loose, doctrinaire, and invective. When Professor Sutherland launched the term, it was applied to those individuals of upper socioeconomic class who violate the criminal law, usually by breach of trust, in the ordinary course of their business activities. This original usage accords with legal ideas of crime and points moreover to the significant and difficult problems of enforcement in the areas of business crimes, particularly where those violations are made criminal by recent statutory enactment. From this fruitful beginning, the term has spread into vacuity, wide and handsome. We learn that the ... existence of such crime may be determined readily "in casual conversation with a representative of an occupation by asking him 'What crooked practices are found in your occupation?'"[42]

Rather oddly—and arguably an unethical move—the editor sent Tappan's paper to Sutherland for review. Sutherland only gently criticized Tappan's manuscript, but he recommended that it not be published. His review read in part:

> Tappan's thesis is: Because criminologists often use the terms "crime" and "criminal" loosely, criminology should be confined to a study of convicted criminals. The first part of this

proposition—that the terms are often used loosely—may be admitted and may be appraised as the author does, as very undesirable. The author does not throw any real light on this part of the proposition and the treatment is in the nature of invective rather than careful scientific analysis. If the first eight pages of the paper had been limited to one paragraph, it would be equally significant. For instance, I should welcome a careful criticism from the legal point of view of the concept of "white-collar crime." The author does not provide this and his statements regarding this concept indicate that he has not read or else not understood my attempt to define the concept in "Is 'White-Collar' Crime?"

Even though the loose usage of these terms were [sic] accepted without qualification, this would provide no justification for the last part of the thesis that convicted criminals are the only justifiable object of study in criminology. No one can have a justifiable objection if some criminologist desires to limit his study to convicted criminals. This is very different from the proposition that all other criminologists should do the same thing. Conviction is important from the point of view of the authority of public agencies to administer punishment. It is not important as a definition of criminal behavior.[43]

In the final paragraph, Sutherland observed that perhaps he should not have agreed to review the article since, if not directly, it implicitly criticized his own work. He said that he had tried to be impersonal and objective, but he recommended to the editor that she solicit opinions from others whose work was not so intimately related to Tappan's theme.[44] It is not known whether she did so, but Tappan's paper, rejected by the *American Journal of Sociology*, was rerouted to the *American Sociological Review*, which published it.

Sutherland was less restrained about Tappan's position in a letter that he sent to Jerome Hall, noting: "My impression is that Tappan is absurd." Sutherland repeated some of the points he had made in his critique of the manuscript. That Hall was not in accord with this sentiment would be evident many years later when he wrote that Tappan's critique was "devastating."[45] Certainly, in at least one regard, Tappan was on target and Sutherland must have sensed this when he noted that he would have welcomed (who besides the saintly really welcome devastating criticism?) a sophisticated legal critique of the concept of white-collar crime. But Tappan undercut what power his position possessed when he went overboard by insisting that the only true criminals were those offenders convicted by the courts, and that criminologists should confine themselves to that group, since the unconvicted but factually guilty possess "no specific membership presently ascertainable,"[46] a rather enigmatic phrase. A person, Tappan maintained, "may be a boor, a sinner, a moral leper, or the devil incarnate, but he does not become a criminal through sociological name-calling unless politically constituted authority says he is."[47] Tappan's argument contains a bit of sleight of hand: the issue is not whether a person is a boor or the devil incarnate; it involves what that person has done. To take but one of many possible examples: would Tappan regard a person as a noncriminal if that person killed seven schoolchildren and then shot himself before any criminal proceedings could be instituted? The ingredients may become more arguable in white-collar offenses, but the fundamental flaw in Tappan's argument remains. Certainly Kreuger, Stavisky, and Musica, all of whom committed suicide when cornered, were self-evidently guilty of offenses that could fall within the territory of studies of white-collar crime. What Tappan probably should have said was that rendering judgments regarding persons who commit what appear to be criminal acts but are not processed through the courts can be an exceedingly difficult task and, though necessary to an effort to truly understand white-collar crime, it needs to be done with great care, the same sort of care that should be involved in determining whether innocent persons have incorrectly been declared by the courts to be criminal, a phenomenon startlingly common as was discovered when DNA testing came into use.

Vilhelm Aubert (1952)

Aubert, a Norwegian sociologist, looked at the issue of defining white-collar crime with an outsider's, that is, a non-American, perspective. This is worth spotlighting because the unchallenged longevity of Sutherland's dicta to a considerable degree was a product of the loyalty that his former students and his colleagues felt toward him in the days when the social science study of crime involved a much smaller and more closely knit

group of scholars than it does today. Aubert thought that Sutherland's formulation had "given rise to futile terminological disputes, which [were]
apt to become clouded by class identifications and ideological convictions."[48] And then he added a rather paradoxical insight that flies in the
face of Tappan's juridical stance:

> For purposes of theoretical analysis, it is of prime importance to
> develop and apply concepts which preserve and emphasize the
> ambiguous nature of the white-collar crimes and not to "solve"
> the problem by classifying them as either "crimes" or "not
> crimes." Their controversial nature is exactly what makes them
> so interesting from a sociological point of view and what gives us
> a clue to important norm conflicts, clashing group interests, and
> maybe incipient social change. One main benefit to be derived
> from the study of white-collar crimes springs from the opportu-
> nity which the ambivalence in the citizen, in the businessman,
> and among lawyers, judges, and even criminologists offers as a
> barometer of structural conflicts and change-potential in the
> larger social system of which they and the white-collar crimes
> are parts.[49]

Aubert went on to report on a study he had conducted in Norway of a
new piece of legislation that regulated the working conditions of domestic
help, a matter which fit into his call for the study of such laws to gain an
understanding of the structural character of a culture. "If those variables
that are mentioned [in this study] are significant causally," Aubert observed in summarizing his work, "it goes once more to show that specific
types of law violations need specific types of explanation."[50] His conclusion may be seen as one log on the polemical fire that would come to dominate theoretical discussions of white-collar crime almost half a century
later in the dispute between general theories and theories attuned to specific patterns of lawbreaking.

Robert G. Caldwell (1958)

Caldwell, a lawyer-sociologist at the University of Iowa, offered what
largely was a recital of Tappan's position. To be considered a criminal one
must be proved so beyond a reasonable doubt. Caldwell granted that there

were miscarriages of justice, but he thought the remedy lay not in disregard of the law's rules to shield the innocent but rather in improvement of the law. He thought that Sutherland had been reasonably restrained in his earliest definitions of white-collar crime, but he balked at the language in Sutherland's criminology textbook, which has been quoted earlier. Caldwell pointed out that some of the acts Sutherland maintained were white-collar crime were not even a violation of the spirit of the law.[51]

My vote on this matter would go to Caldwell. Unless we use a taut definition of harm, a most difficult task, it seems feckless to seek to determine acts that *should* be crimes and to amalgamate their perpetrators with persons who violate explicit statutes. Of course, it is a perfectly sensible enterprise to learn things about such unproscribed acts and those who commit them, but it would seem to be fouling criminological waters by incorporating such ventures into the discipline's bailiwick.

Herbert Edelhertz (1970)

Herbert Edelhertz, trained at the University of Michigan Law School, was chief of the fraud section of the federal Department of Justice when he was funded by the Law Enforcement Assistance Administration to examine the realm of white-collar crime. The result was a definition that drew exclusively upon legal precepts and, as Edelhertz noted, differed markedly from Sutherland's approach, but which previewed the stand that would be taken decades later in the influential work by scholars headquartered in the Yale Law School. Edelhertz thought that Sutherland's definition was far too restrictive. "White-collar crime is democratic," Edelhertz asserted, "and can be committed by a bank clerk or the head of his institution."[52] He proposed that a more useful definition would be "an illegal act or series of illegal acts committed by nonphysical means and by concealment or guile, to obtain money or property, to avoid the payment or loss or money or property, or to obtain business or personal advantage."[53] He set out four subdivisions to embrace what he regarded as white-collar crime: (1) crimes by persons operating on an individual, ad hoc basis, for personal gain in a nonbusiness context; (2) crimes in the course of their occupations by those operating inside businesses, government, or other establishments, or in a professional capacity, in violation of their duty of loyalty and fidelity to employer or client; (3) crimes incidental to and in furtherance of business operations, but not the central purpose of such business operations; and (4) white-collar crime as a business, or as the central activity of the business. The last, Edelhertz indicated, referred to outlawed confidence games.[54]

Criticisms of the Edelhertz formulation came from social scientists who quarreled with various of its elements. For one thing, they thought it unnecessarily verbose with a tendency, characteristic of much legalese, to throw in anything that might conceivably be relevant rather than to cut to the core.[55] Why, for instance, is there the phrase "a series of acts," when one act alone is all that is needed to meet the definition? Why the focus on motive, which is not required to be proven in an American criminal court, and which often is not an obvious matter, even to the offender? Why include con games? Most particularly, Edelhertz's work suffered from a failure to illustrate his various categories with specific examples of what he had in mind. It is not clear, for instance, where Edelhertz stood on the matter of formal criminal court adjudication of an act as requisite for declaring it to be a white-collar crime.

Critics were puzzled by Edelhertz's exclusion of violence form the realm of white-collar crime, noting that offenses such as unnecessary surgical operations, the knowing manufacture and marketing of unsafe automobiles, and the failure to label poisonous substances in the workplace could be regarded as white-collar crimes with a strong component of violence. Miriam Saxon, for instance, in challenging Edelhertz's formulation, pointed out that the MER/29 case involved a pharmaceutical corporation that knowingly sold an anticholesterol drug that subjected at least 5,000 people to such serious side effects as cataracts and hair loss.[56] She believed that the company's behavior reasonably could be regarded as an act of violence. A left-leaning attorney left no doubt about how he felt regarding violence as an attribute of white-collar crime: "I don't defend right-wing murderers," he said in a newspaper interview. "If I wanted to defend right-wing murderers, I'd become a corporate lawyer."[57] And lest there be any doubt that in the public imagination white-collar crime includes acts of violence, a full-page advertisement in the April 21, 2005, issue of the New York Times for Joseph Finder's Company Man, a novel about the actions of the CEO of a Michigan corporation, proclaimed in one-inch high red letters: WHITE/COLLAR/CRIME ISN'T/ALWAYS/ BLOODLESS.

The American Bar Association would largely adopt Edelhertz's definition, although preferring the term "economic offenses" to "white-collar
crimes." The Association also deftly modified the term "nonviolent" with
the footnoted observation that this referred specifically to the means by
which the crime is committed, though they granted that "the harm to the
society can frequently be described as violent." [58] It is a bit strange to focus
on harm to the society, rather than on the injury inflicted on the victim.
But this hair-splitting distinction lines up with the recent Supreme Court
observation, based on statutory law, that "a crime of violence involves the
use of physical force against another's person or property." The court
added: "While one may, in theory, actively employ *something* in an acci-
dental manner, it is much less natural to say that a person employs physical
force against another by accident."[59] It may be "less natural" to linguisti-
cally designate the action as violent, but it can be argued that if the actor
was careless or negligent it would not seem unreasonable to classify an
injury to a person or property as a result of violence.

Elements of both Edelhertz's and Sutherland's formulations appeared
in a crime terminology dictionary issued in 1981 by the Bureau of Justice
Statistics in the Department of Justice that sought to cover all bases and
ended up as something of a stew. If anything, this attempt only further
confused the issue.

> White-collar crime is nonviolent crime for financial gain com-
> mitted by means of deception by persons whose occupational
> status is entrepreneurial, professional or semi-professional and
> utilizing their special occupational skills and opportunities;
> also, nonviolent crime for financial gain utilizing deception and
> committed by anyone having special technical or professional
> knowledge of business and government, irrespective of the
> person's occupation.[60]

Harold Pepinsky (1974)

Harold Pepinsky of Indiana University, something of a polymath (he has
a sociology Ph.D., a law degree, and is fluent in Chinese and Norwegian,
among other skills) attempted to rebut Tappan's attack on Sutherland's
position and to reformulate that position. He argued that Sutherland's
definition, rather than being too broad, was not broad enough. For

Pepinsky, the key ingredient of the behavior that criminology had sorely neglected was the phenomenon of "exploitation," which he believed should supersede the idea of white-collar crime because the concept of exploitation allegedly was socioeconomically unbiased and conceptually unitary. Pepinsky maintained that Sutherland was on firm ground when he ignored the distinction between civil and criminal cases since the two approaches "do not differentiate wrongs by seriousness."[61] He pointed out that civil trials may have higher standards of proof than criminal trials because the civil trial doctrine of "preponderance of evidence" tends to be adhered to much more rigidly than the criminal trial criterion of "beyond a reasonable doubt." Pepinsky also observed that some things treated as white-collar crimes, such as antitrust violations, could not reasonably be regarded as socially injurious, a debatable and much-debated view.

Pepinsky explains his position in these terms:

> The reformulated definition is based on the social injury caused by all acts of exploitation. Manifestly, exploitation can include many acts other than those that have been considered white-collar crimes. Anything called a crime against private property would come under the rubric of exploitation. Exploitation would cover a sale of a product to a customer who expressed the belief that the quality of the product is less than he thought he paid for. Failure of a government to accept a producer's request to amend a defense contract because of allegedly unforeseen expenses would be exploitation. . . . An unchallenged use of private property is not exploitation, nor can exploitation b e applied to the use of other than private property.[62]

Essentially, what Pepinsky seemed to be declaring was that exploitation involved the continuing possession of unused private property that another reasonably sought to use. An example offered was of a man vacationing who owned a vacuum cleaner that his neighbor desired to use. If the vacationer was himself using the vacuum, all was well; if he planned to use it sometime in the future and refused to allow his neighbor to use it at that moment, this was exploitation. Thus, private property refers to "a resource over which user attempts to hold dominion, on any basis other than immediate personal need for the use, against a request for use by another."[63] For Pepinsky, utopia was a place in which all property was held in common. Pepinsky's contribution represents a blip on the screen of attempts to pin down an acceptable definition of white-collar crime, interesting for its reach and distinctiveness, but having had no impact on research or theory during the three decades since it originally was enunciated.

Lest Pepinsky appear to be merely a strange and lone voice supporting an odd idea, it can be noted that the eminent seventeenth century political philosopher John Locke maintained that if property remained unused, it should be taken up and assigned to someone who wuld make use of it.[64]

Leonard Orland (1980)

The most powerful critique of Sutherland's position from a legal viewpoint is that of Leonard Orland, a University of Connecticut law professor who has specialized in the study of corporate wrongdoing. Unlike Tappan and Caldwell, Orland went into extensive and specific detail regarding what he regarded as the abysmal shortcomings and errors in Sutherland's work. And unlike them, since he was housed solely in a law school, Orland was not constrained by the implicit rules of etiquette and self-protection that assuredly tempered the reservations expressed about Sutherland's contribution by Tappan and Caldwell. At the same time, the impact of Orland's position for criminologists was undercut by the fact that, unlike the articles by Tappan and Caldwell, which were published in mainstream social science outlets, Orland's appeared in a law journal, where it was much less likely to be discovered and absorbed by white-collar crime scholars.

Orland used tough words to express his disdain of what he saw as Sutherland's high-handed and irresponsible labeling of so wide a variety of violations as criminal acts. He focused on Sutherland's discussion of corporate misdeeds and argued that it and the remainder of the nonlegal literature on the subject was "hopelessly misguided"[65] and that it suffered from "enormous theoretical and methodological deficiencies."[66] This broadside included a complementary disparagement of a government publication by Marshall Clinard and colleagues that Orland thought employed a definition of corporate crime that was even more amiss than Sutherland's. The Clinard research team had maintained that "corporate crime includes any act punished by the state, regardless of whether it is punished under administrative, civil, or criminal law. . . . Any definition of crime, therefore, solely in terms of criminal law is restrictive for an adequate understanding of corporate crime."[67] Despite the "massive flaws" in Sutherland's work, Orland observed, "it continues to be . . . revered in the sociological community."[68] To deal adequately with white-collar crime, he noted, requires sophistication in a broad range of technical areas of the law, a quality that he felt that Sutherland sorely lacked.

Orland granted that there were acts that truly ought to be regarded as crimes that were missed, ignored, or dealt with otherwise. But he emphasized that behavior that in no manner could be seen as criminal, either in law or common sense, were considered to be white-collar crimes in Sutherland's examination of the records of corporate behavior. In American law, for instance, false advertising is regarded as a tort to be dealt with primarily by cease-and-desist orders or in civil courts. The same is true of copyright and infringement laws, counted by Sutherland, but never considered in law as serious wrongs. Orland noted that only 159 of the 980 adverse decisions against corporations that Sutherland defined as criminal acts had been dealt with by criminal courts, and that many were handled by administrative agencies that did not possess criminal jurisdiction.

Orland's persuasive point that an offense such as false advertising is a civil matter and not a crime is particularly noteworthy. Sutherland in his 1949 book had a field day at the expense of corporations that had illegally puffed their wares, devoting an entire chapter to "Misrepresentation in Advertising." He noted that the Pure Food and Drug Act of 1906 had decreed that misrepresentations on product labels could be prosecuted as crime. Then he observed that the 1914 Act establishing the Federal Trade Commission (FTC) had placed false advertising under the Commission's jurisdiction. Sutherland, however, never explicitly pointed out that the FTC statute does not make false advertising a crime, observing only that the Commission uses cease-and-desist orders against those it deems are misrepresenting their wares. Sutherland offered a roster of companies selling commonly used products that had been told to clean up their advertising act—a roster that included twenty-eight of the sixty-nine large corporations he studied that used advertisements for sales purposes. He offered a litany of misrepresentations, including "'alligator shoes' that are not made with alligator hides and 'walnut furniture' which is not made from walnut lumber."[69] Sutherland sought to smuggle these offenses into the "white-collar crime" category by comparing them to a Chicago case in which two con men were imprisoned for selling a concoction of water with an aspirin dissolved in it to a blind man, claiming that it would cure him of his malady. One had to wonder whether Sutherland was unable to resist a good lode of muckraking material, even though it challenged the integrity of the acceptable range of his stipulated subject matter.

The Yale Law School Project (1982–1991)

By far, the most significant revisionist move against Sutherland's focus on social position as a key ingredient in white-collar crime emerged from a decade-long series of studies by a prominent group of scholars headed by sociologist Stanton Wheeler and housed in the law school at Yale University.[70] The research team was subsidized by a well-funded and broadly defined commission from the National Institute of Justice. The researchers' law school setting, and the demands of the research task, led them to reformulate the concept of white-collar crime in terms of federal statutory provisions. This permitted them to get a hold on bounded data—that is, all the prosecuted cases in a particular federal jurisdiction that came under a designated penal code provision. They could then employ this data to determine the characteristics of the offenders in each statutory category as well as other elements of the total sample, such as recidivism rates and sentencing patterns.

After combing the statute books, the Yale group settled upon eight federal offenses that they believed represented the range of white-collar crime. These were securities fraud, antitrust violations, bribery, tax offenses, bank embezzlement, postal and wire fraud, false claims and statements, and credit- and lending-institution fraud. They then sampled persons in seven federal district courts who had been convicted of these offenses. They also were given access to the presentence reports of probation officers, which contained information about the perpetrators. They concentrated exclusively on criminal cases, deciding not to embrace either civil decisions or administrative actions.

The key dispute regarding the Yale approach was whether they were truly studying what the scholarly field traditionally had regarded as white-collar crime or whether they were opening up another realm of inquiry, albeit assuredly one that offered considerably greater opportunity for the kinds of statistical sophistication that criminology had come to particularly value. Kathleen Daly, a participant in the Yale team's work, examining the women in the study sample, concluded that it was "occupational marginality" that best characterized their vocational standing. Virtually all of the female bank embezzlers in her sample, for instance, were clerical workers, and as many as a third in some offense categories were unemployed. In an aside, Daly mused: "The women's socioeconomic profile, coupled with the nature of their crimes, makes one wonder if 'white-collar' aptly describes them or their illegalities."[71] One writer, tongue-in-cheek, portrayed female law violators such as these as "frayed-collar criminals."[72] For the men, 7.2 percent of the total were unemployed at the time they violated the law. In the categories of credit fraud, false claims, and mail fraud, fewer than half of the offenders were said to be "steadily employed" and more than half of the mail fraud offenders were unemployed at the time of their offense.

The Yale definition of white-collar crime provided impetus to a considerable range of research probes, several of them taking issue with Sutherland's conclusions, though not acknowledging that what Sutherland had established was germane to his sample and what they had found was the consequence of a quite different study population. The Yale team, for instance, concluded that white-collar offenders were sentenced more severely than traditional offenders.[73] A polemical note intruded into the subtitle of the report—"Rhetoric and Reality?"—with its message that Sutherland's position that white-collar offenders were dealt with leniently by the courts was "rhetoric" and their finding was the "reality." But the true reality was that they had reached their conclusions on the basis of a sample significantly different from Sutherland's. The great importance of this consideration was exemplified by a research probe by John Hagan and Patricia Parker that used the Sutherland criteria to distinguish offenders. Its results supported Sutherland and contradicted the Yale Law School team position.[74] So did a review of the sentences levied against health care providers convicted of violating the provisions of California's Medi-Cal program.[75]

Another study based on the Yale sample reported that white-collar offenders recidivate at about the same rate as other criminals, contrary to what Sutherland had suggested.[76] Such a conclusion might not have held up if the study sample had been confined to the likes of Exxon and Adelphia executives and other contemporary offenders from the upper echelons of the corporate world.

David Weisburd and several of the stalwarts of the Yale project encapsulated their major findings in a book titled *Crimes of the Middle Classes*. In truth, the people studied came from all social classes, not exclusively from the middle class. The book's major theme was that Sutherland was wrong in considering white-collar crime as elite behavior; that the perpetrators could be found on other social levels. "Empirical studies," the authors wrote, "suggest that much of what has been assumed to be white-collar crime is committed by people in the middle class rather than the upper classes of our society."[77]

The sentence is clearly misleading. Sutherland specifically defined white-collar criminals as upper-class offenders. A definition such as Sutherland's cannot be in error, although it very well may not be as useful as other approaches for either theoretical and research purposes. In this regard, the Yale definition clearly enjoys the advantage. But its semantic quarrel with Sutherland's idea of white-collar crime might have been avoided had the Yale team pinned a different label on its study population and not pressed the idea that they were studying what truly was the "real" realm of white-collar crime. It might also have bene useful if they had separated out offenders in their sample who fit Sutherland's definition—perhaps about one-quarter of the total—and provided data about these people.

As a note in the *Harvard Law Review* points out, "Had the authors limited their definition to offenses such as antitrust and securities violations (crimes in which higher status offenders are more prevalent), the study might have yielded substantially different results." [78]

Note, They could on this basis have offered results congruent with the then-prevailing definition of white-collar crime. Some justification for such an approach appears in their finding that "officers and managers commit [crimes] inflicting the most harm,"[79] to which might have been added "and therefore may merit separate consideration."

Instead, a certain self-fulfilling prophecy was employed: "[W]ere we to narrow the scope of white-collar crime research to the most elite white-collar criminals," it was said, "we would exclude the bulk of those people who are convicted for so-called white-collar offenses."[80] The key word here is "so-called." The authors themselves had pinned the label on the offenses they specified, and then reified their own maneuver to support this conclusion. Another way of addressing the same issue could just as well have been: "Since we have extended the scope of white-collar crime well beyond its original formulation, the bulk of people who are convicted of the offenses we have chosen to examine traditionally would not have been considered white-collar criminals." It would have been a good opportunity to coin a new word or phrase to encompass their study population. Indeed, the original term "white-collar crime," whatever its referents, is now something of a misnomer as presidents and prime ministers—and numerous others in the elite classes—often wear sports clothes while carrying on their work, not to mention the apparel worn by the increasing number of women in high places in the world of work.

Susan Shapiro (1990)

A strong call to reconceptualize white-collar crime—or, as she termed it, to "liberate" the term—has been offered by Susan Shapiro, a member of the Yale group, who insisted it ought to refer specifically and only to violations of trust that allow persons "to rob without violence and and burgle without trespass."[81] Shapiro endorses the idea that white-collar crime ought to be defined in terms of the behavior, not the violator: "it is time to integrate 'white-collar' offenders into mainstream scholarship by looking beyond the perpetrators' wardrobe and social characteristics and exploring the modus operandi of their misdeeds," Shapiro states.[82] She seeks to pinpoint the kinds of behavior that she believes belong in the white-collar crime realm and specifies the generic category of violations of trust rather than of specific laws. Violators of trust are seen as persons who manipulate norms of disclosure, disinterest, and role competence. Their acts involve matters such as misrepresentation, self-dealing, corruption, and role conflict. As a whimsical example of misrepresentation, Shapiro relates the story of what she calls "Zoogate"—that the zoo in Houston advertised live cobras but actually displayed rubber replicas, since cobras could not live under the lights in the area where they would have to be kept.

Prosecution of crimes involving abuse of trust is handicapped, Shapiro notes, because of the ambiguity that makes for unknowing victims—that is, persons who never become aware that they have been duped—and by the fact that suspects tend to have custody of the critical evidence against them. She grants that the Sutherland heritage is not easily cast aside, because it is "politically powerful" and "palpably self-evident."[83] She also grants that her redesign of the concept has some problems; for instance, it excludes antitrust crimes as well as corporate violence. Nonetheless, Shapiro concludes with a resounding indictment of the Sutherland approach to white-collar crime, which she says

> created an imprisoning framework for contemporary scholarship, impoverishing theory, distorting empirical inquiry, oversimplifying policy analysis, inflaming our muckraking instincts, and obscuring fascinating questions about the relationships between social organization and crime.[84]

Perhaps the most intriguing observation regarding Shapiro's call for a reformulation of white-collar crime is from David Friedrichs, who indicates that the value of the concept as Sutherland enunciated it is that it alerts scholars and laypersons to the phenomenon with which it deals. "If white collar criminologists treat white collar crime as dispassionately and as neutrally as Shapiro seems to want them to do, then perhaps they effectively concede to major corporations and other elite segments disproportionate power to continue to shape public perceptions of crime."[85]

WHITE-COLLAR CRIME THEORY

The category of white-collar crime has since the concept's first enunciation been the graveyard of theories that offer an explanation of all criminal behavior. Sutherland put to rest the then-current views that feeblemindedness, immigrant status, and Freudian complexes could account for all forms of lawbreaking, since they clearly did not fit with white-collar offenses. To avoid this quagmire, James Q. Wilson and Richard Herrnstein exempted white-collar offenses from their concerns, suggesting that they were a different kind of behavior than "real" crime which for them involves predatory street offenses.[86] Theories that have come into play since Sutherland's time typically have confined themselves to juvenile delinquency and street crimes and avoided notice of white-collar and corporate offenses.

Nonetheless, several theoretical constructs have ventured to include white-collar crime within their embrace, and one, by James W. Coleman, has been aimed at explaining only white-collar crime. We will examine four major statements that bear on the interpretation of white-collar crime.

Edwin H. Sutherland (1939)

We have already met with Sutherland's theory of differential association put forward in his presidential address as offering the best explanation of white-collar crime. The theory was initially enunciated in the first chapter of the 1939 edition of Sutherland's textbook, *Principles of Criminology*. He presented a revised formulation in the 1947 edition, altering the claim that the theory explained only "systematic" behavior to the position that it could account for all criminal behavior. We need only itemize the nine points of the theory to show that its adequacy is well beyond demonstration or refutation. The postulates are these:

1. Criminal behavior is leaned; it is not inherited.
2. Criminal behavior is learned in interaction with other persons in a process of communication.
3. The principal part of the learning of criminal behavior occurs within intimate personal groups. Impersonal agencies of communication, such as motion pictures and newspapers, play a relatively unimportant part in the genesis of criminal behavior.
4. When criminal behavior is learned, the learning includes (a) techniques of committing the crime, which are sometimes very complicated, sometimes very simple; (b) the specific direction of motives, drives, rationalizations, and attitudes.
5. The specific direction of motives and drives is learned from the definition of legal codes as favorable or unfavorable. In American society, these definitions are almost always mixed, and consequently we have culture conflict in relation to the legal codes.

6. A person becomes delinquent because of an excess of definitions favorable to violation of the law over definitions unfavorable to violation of the law. This is the principle of differential
association.

7. Differential associations may vary in frequency, duration, pri-
ority, and intensity.

8. The process of learning criminal behavior by association with
criminal and anticriminal patterns involves all of the mecha-
nisms that are involved in any other learning.

9. Though criminal behavior is an expression of general needs and
values, it is not explained by these general needs and values
since noncriminal behavior is an expression of the same needs
and values. Thieves generally steal in order to secure money,
but likewise honest laborers work in order to secure money. The
attempts by many criminologists to explain criminal behavior
by general drives and values, such as the happiness principle,
striving for social status, the money motive, or frustration, have
been and must continue to be futile since they explain lawful
behavior as completely as they explain criminal behavior.[87]

It is uncertain whether the theory was originally designed as a peda-
gogical tool in order to provide students with a framework or sense of order
by which to look at the diversified forms of crime or whether Sutherland
espoused differential association as a full-grown theory that might lend
itself to testing. Donald Cressey, in an article detailing the strengths and
inadequacies of differential association, concluded that it ought best be regarded as a principle rather than a theory that could put the development of
behavior into some logical pattern. Cressey observed that a theory attempts
to establish an explanatory framework within which subhypotheses and
predictive statements can be made; differential association falls short of
this desideratum.[88] Cressey also took issue with Sutherland's theory in his
classic study of embezzlers, insisting that persons who embezzle are perfectly aware of how to steal money and need no prompting from association with those who might teach them techniques or rationalizations.[89]

It is surprising, looking back, that sophisticated scholars did not
throw up their hands in despair when confronted with the differential association theory. It takes no great understanding to appreciate at once

that many of its ingredients are beyond any possible empirical demonstration; or, as Anthony Harris sarcastically commented: "Differential association . . . bears little risk of falsification."[90] Solomon Kobrin has pointed out that even delinquents growing up in a depressed urban area are exposed to a huge input of both criminal and normative cues in highly complex degrees and arrangements.[91] How can such experiences possibly be untangled and tallied as "favorable" or "unfavorable?"

Criminologists in the United States have taken differential association quite seriously—and some still do, though they reformulate and corrupt the postulates into different, but workable, designs; for example, by counting the number of criminal friends a person has as a proxy for the learning process outlined by Sutherland.[92] Foreign scholars, however, not constrained by Sutherland's preeminent standing in the field, have been much less impressed by differential association. John Barton Mays, a Scotsman, believed that the theory was "inadequate and unsubtle." It "takes us a little way," he wrote, "and then abandons us to doubt."[93] Nigel Walker, a professor at Cambridge University in England, wrote that differential association and many other theories of crime "begin with the observation of the obvious, generalize it into a principle, and are eventually reduced again to a statement of the limited truths from which they originated."[94] Sir Leon Radzinowicz, Polish-born, later head of the Institute of Criminology at Cambridge, thought that the tenets of differential association were "difficult to accept" and constituted "broad platitudes."[95] John Braithwaite, an Australian, granted that Sutherland's propositions might be correct, but that "unless they are given some specificity, they will remain banal, untestable and of limited use for testing policy."[96]

James W. Coleman (1987)

James W. Coleman gathered together signposts in the research and pinpointed significant gaps in our knowledge about white-collar crime in what he designated as a unified integrated theoretical framework. Coleman observed that "[t]aken as a whole, the literature on the etiology and development of white-collar crime is a hodge-podge of studies looking at different crimes from different levels of analysis."[97] For his part, he focused especially on two conditions that he said offered theoretical insight into white-collar crime: the confluence of appropriate motivation and opportunity. Like all the white-collar crime theories, this one could, without much tweaking, be declared to "explain" all human behavior, a conclusion that no social scientist is likely to take seriously. For Coleman, motivation for white-collar crime is associated with the social structure of industrial capitalism and the culture of competition to which it has given rise. He quotes the following observation in support of his position:

> [M]uch criminal activity is responsive to the kinds of things for which we stand. Individualism, hedonism, materialism—these are criminogenic social values: they may have utility for the production of many social and individual boons; and they may be preferable on some grounds to different social emphases. But they have their price, and part of that price clearly appears to be the phenomenon of white-collar crime.[98]

This thesis is seconded in a recent treatise that insists that Americans today are driven addicts living turbocharged lives in pursuit of status and possessions. The author focuses on what he sees as an outbreak of greed in the business world in which people who have no need of extra money nonetheless will scheme and cheat to obtain it.[99]

Coleman points out that in preindustrial times there was not enough surplus wealth to breed competitive behavior. He defines motivation as "a set of symbolic constructions, defining certain kinds of goals and activities as appropriate and desirable and others as lacking those qualities."[100] This is not far different from Sutherland's designation of attitudes toward the law as a key ingredient of illegal behavior. While motivation so defined might be determined after an act, it is arguable how satisfactorily it could be used in an attempt to predict an act, except in the sense that, for instance, someone who believes that smoking pot is perfectly appropriate can reasonably be presumed more likely than someone with the opposite view to smoke marijuana.[101] The same shortcoming in terms of the possibility of scientific demonstration is true of the definition of opportunity, which is said to be a circumstance regarded as attractive or unattractive from the standpoint of a particular individual. Coleman's vision of opportunity has four components:

> The first is the actor's perception of how great a gain he or she might expect to reap from the opportunity. Second is the

perception of potential risks, such as the likelihood that the criminal act will be detected and the severity of the sanctions that would be invoked if detection indeed occurs. The third factor is the compatibility of the opportunity with the ideas, rationalizations, and beliefs the individual actor already has. Finally, the evaluation of an illicit opportunity is made in comparison with the other opportunities of which the actor is aware.[102]

Coleman's broad interpretative sweep is useful in calling attention to ingredients that particularly seem to characterize white-collar crime, which he defines much as Sutherland had. But his theorizing lacks parsimony, that is, the concise neatness that is considered to be a desirable characteristic of sophisticated theoretical statements. It also suffers from an absence of a catchy title, such as "differential association." Such labels help considerably to promote theories in the competitive marketplace of intellectual ideas.

Michael Gottfredson and Travis Hirschi (1990)

White-collar (but not corporate) crime is directly addressed by Michael Gottfredson and Travis Hirschi in what during the last years of the previous century and the initial years of the present one has stood out as the most prominent theoretical construct in American criminology. In their monograph *A General Theory of Crime*, Gottfredson and Hirschi state that the absence of self-control, combined with opportunity, is adequate to explain all crime at all times and in all places,[103] as well as analogous "deviant acts" such as "accidents, victimizations, truancies from home, school, and work, substance abuse, family problems, and disease,"[104] along with the tendency to "smoke, use drugs, have children out of wedlock, and engage in illicit sex."[105] People with low self-control are said to be risk-seeking, short-sighted, insensitive to others, and to desire immediate gratification. Crime is an ordinary act that requires "no skill, no organization, no resources, no success. . . . The offender sees a momentary opportunity to get something for nothing and siezes [sic] it."[106] White-collar crime specifically is declared to "provide relatively quick, relatively certain benefit with minimum effort."[107] These characteristics conflict with any long-term commitment to work, friendships, marriage, and family life. Criminals are ecumenical in the offenses that they commit, not limiting themselves to any particular form of lawbreaking. Self-control is (or is not) acquired early in life through effective child-rearing practices. Consequently, low self-control is a product of poor parental monitoring of a child's behavior, lack of parental recognition of ill omens, and/or ineffective discipline for transgressions.

An outpouring of research studies have sought to test the accuracy of self-control theory. Invariably, they conclude that there is indeed a partial connection between illegal behavior and absence of self-control in the perpetrator. Critics maintain that this is self-evident. They argue that the illegal and analogous behaviors that are claimed to be explained by the theory are regarded as undesirable because they are characterized by an absence of self-control in a society which, as do virtually all societies, finds acts demonstrating lack of self-control unpalatable, particularly if they result in harm to others. In this regard, the theory is regarded as tautological; the answer is the same as the question. Question: What causes acts that are marked by an lack of self-control? Answer: A lack of self-control. Gottfredson and Hirschi seek to refute this view by noting that they are proud of the allegation of tautology. "In our view," they write, "the charge of tautology is in fact a compliment; an assertion that we followed the path of logic in producing an internally consistent result."[108] It is doubtful that many scientists would agree: the aim is not an "internally consistent" result but a product that produces knowledge that meshes with external realities.

In their attempt to incorporate white-collar crime into their theoretical kingdom, Gottfredson and Hirschi initially had to face the question which we dealt with earlier in this chapter: what is to be regarded as white-collar crime? In their general discussion of the subject, they talk of white-collar crimes as acts committed by "the rich and the powerful."[109] But when they seek to incorporate the behavior into their theoretical framework, it is the Uniform Crime Report categories of fraud, forgeries, and embezzlement that they rely upon. As Darrell Steffensmeier has pointed out, these rubrics cover behavior that is not primarily occupation related bur rather involves acts such as passing bad checks, credit card fraud, identification falsification, defrauding an innkeeper, fraudulent use of public transportation, and welfare fraud.[110] Nonetheless, Gottfredson and Hirschi offer a particularly forceful and key statement on why they regard white-collar crime as just another form of illegal activity:

> Yet what is the theoretical value in distinguishing a pharmacist's theft of drugs from a carpenter's theft of lumber? What is the theoretical value in distinguishing a doctor's Medicaid fraud from a patient's Medicaid fraud? What is the theoretical value of distinguishing a bank manager's embezzlement from a service-station attendant's embezzlement? The white-collar crime concept tends to suggest that the pharmacist's theft is more important or serious than, or the product of different causes from, the carpenter's theft. It suggests that the doctor's fraud is more important (socially damaging?) or serious than the patient's, that the causes of one differ from the causes of the other. And so on. It strikes us that these suggestions are problematic at best and really involve two, largely unrelated but often confused questions: Are the causes of various offenses the same? And, Are the offenses themselves equally serious? White-collar theorists and researchers (in common with many criminologists) often assume that the answer to the second question bears on the answer to the first; that is, more serious crimes must have causes different from (more powerful than?) those of less serious crimes. Certainly there is no logical requirement that causes of offenses somehow match their seriousness, and, as we shall show, there is good empirical evidence that they do not and good theoretical reasons why they should not.[111]

For argumentative purposes this is a tactically shrewd and in terms of debating skills a very sophisticated paragraph. Its basic problem is that it frames the issue in a way that leads a reader to the conclusion that the writers desire, but, while doing so, essentially sidesteps the vulnerable aspects of the theory as it pertains to white-collar crime. Gottfredson and Hirschi's core position that seriousness fails to offer theoretical substance for differentiating suite from street crimes would seem irrefutable. What is refutable, and not addressed in the paragraph, is whether an absence of self-control plus opportunity makes any sense in regard to occupational crimes of the rich and powerful.

Scholars aplenty have offered critiques that insisted that self-control theory fails to provide a satisfactory explanation of the behavior of men (and much fewer women) who have reached the pinnacle of success through the demonstration of self-control prior to having embarked on illegal acts.[112] Their lives had been marked by the postponement of gratification, self-interested calculation and restraint; in short, they got where they were by means of self-controlled behavior. Nor by any stretch could they be regarded as polymorphous perverse; that is, as antitrust violators who also commit burglary and robbery among a myriad of other kinds of offenses.

Commentators have used insider trading as an exemplar when discussing what they regard as the inaccuracy of the absence of crime specialization in self-control theory. Kenneth Polk noted that Gottfredson and Hirschi's general theory "would tell us that criminals do not specialize in one form of crime, that today's burglar is yesterday's insider trader and tomorrow's rapist." Polk then asks: "Is this actually true for insider traders?" He points out that people such as Ivan Boesky,[113] Dennis Levine,[114] and Michael Milken[115] obviously concentrated on financial crimes and that their illegal behaviors were not interchangeable with street offenses.[116]

Gottfredson and Hirschi themselves offer some fuel to critics when they reenter the decades-old Cressey-Sutherland debate about embezzlement. They note that Cressey had thought that reducing opportunities and changing the business ethos would be a useful tactic to reduce embezzling. They differ: "In our version, embezzlement can be prevented by reducing opportunity and by hiring employees or managers who have been adequately socialized to generally accepted values both inside and outside the business world that forbid stealing."[117] That policy formula sounds rather like Sutherland's view that unfavorable attitudes toward the law is a key consideration in lawbreaking, not the absence of self-control.

In addition, note can be taken of a study of savings and loan swindles that concluded that what was learned "moves in exactly the opposite direction of Gottfredson and Hirschi's theoretical position by suggesting that many forms of white-collar crime are not reducible to individuals and their characteristics, but are embedded in large institutional and organizational arrangements."[118]

Gottfredson and Hirschi had rejected the tactic of Wilson and Herrnstein, who confined their theorizing to predatory street crimes. This is the way Wilson and Herrnstein stated their case:

> The word "crime" can be applied to such varied behavior that it is not clear that it is a meaningful category of analysis. Stealing a comic book, punching a friend, robbing a bank, bribing a politician, hijacking an airplane—these and countless other acts are all crimes. Crime is as broad a category as disease, and perhaps as useless.[119]

Wilson and Herrnstein thought it feckless to compare persons who park by fire hydrants to persons who rob banks. Gottfredson and Hirschi, who even incorporate disease under their umbrella, wonder why Wilson and Herrnstein took an opposite position "without clear evidence that such restriction is necessary."[120] The shoals upon which self-control theory appears to break up when it is applied to white-collar offenses of the rich and powerful may offer such evidence. Jack Katz has suggested a set of circumstances that challenge self-control theory. A man each evening walks by a closed jewelry store. He does so for months, then suddenly breaks the window and steals some bracelets and watches. Presumably his level of self-control has not altered during that period, nor has the opportunity varied. More generally, as Katz puts the matter: "[A] reliance for explanation on background determinism had made twentieth-century social theory fundamentally incapable of comprehending the causation of white-collar crime."[121]

Neal Shover and Andy Hochstetler (2006)

The most recent systematic attempt to interpret white-collar crime within a particular theoretical framework appears in the work of Neal Shover and Andy Hochstetler, who rely upon the concept of rational choice to seek to explain the dynamics that underlie white-collar offenses. They write:

> The closing decades of the 20th-century saw dramatic change in the way policy makers and elite academics talk about crime and what should be done about it. In place of deterministic explanations of the sources that had enjoyed support for decades, they now argue that criminal choices are preceded by

a decision-making process in which individuals assess options and their potential net payoffs, paying attention particularly to potential aversive consequences. When viewed through the lens of crime-as-choice theory, crime unambiguously is purposeful and calculated action.[122]

Rational choice precepts found their way into theorizing about crime through the work of economists who seek to comprehend in marketplace terms how human behavior works and how it might be changed. Simply put, rational choice theory says that humans are goal-oriented (with money being a particularly powerful goal) and that their behavior can be manipulated by changing situations so that acts that violate the law will not have satisfying outcomes.

Rational choice theory has become deeply embedded in social science research in fields adjacent to the study of crime. In 1957, for instance, there was no mention of the theory in political science journals, but today almost half of the articles in these journals are built around rational choice premises.

Most rational choice theorists appreciate that at best they are supporting an approach that is a sensitizing principle; that is, it suggests things that you probably ought to look at if you are trying to understand such matters as white-collar crime. The two major items to consider are what the person who did the act sought to achieve and what that person believed were the circumstances that would enable him or her to get away with the outlawed behavior. Derek Cornish and Ronald Clarke, the leading criminological exponents of the rational choice approach, are well aware of the complications associated with its ingredients:

> Offenders seek to benefit themselves by their criminal behavior. This involves the making of decisions and choices, however rudimentary on occasion these processes might be. These processes exhibit a measure of rationality, albeit constrained by limits of time and the availability of relevant information.[123]

Cornish and Clarke observe that we must stop looking at crime as a single kind of behavior and instead focus on specific behavioral forms. Closer attention must be paid to the particular criminal event itself and to the situational conditions that played into its occurrence. This view echoes the conclusion of the President's Commission on Law Enforcement and Administration of Justice that maintained that "Each crime is a response to a specific situation by a party with an infinitely complicated psychological and emotional makeup who is subject to infinitely complicated external pressures" and that, therefore, "the causes of crime are numerous and mysterious and intertwined."[124]

Beyond the fact that "different folks respond to different strokes," rational choice theory is faced with the problem of reaching into the brain of the individual offender as that person calculates how much he or she feels the need for things that can be secured from white-collar crimes: things such as money, peer acclaim, excitement, promotion, and challenge. Nor are we altogether similar in the risks that we are willing to run, as a look at hang-gliding enthusiasts, auto racers, boxers, and cowards will quickly demonstrate. In addition, individuals may at times follow the dictates of moral codes and do things that apparently are not in their own self-interest. Finally, the theory offers no particular insight into how interests arise and how and why they change. That said, it must also be noted that rational choice theorists tend to be pragmatic: they make no grandiose claims for the theory but point out that it offers some worthwhile understanding in a general way of why human beings act as they do.

To conclude, we might best quote the observation of Robert Nisbet that briefly encapsulates some major concerns that this chapter documents. He writes:

> Beyond a certain point, it is a waste of time to seek the semantic justifications for concepts used by creative minds. The important and all-too-often neglected task in philosophy and social theory is that of observing the ways in which abstract concepts are converted by their creators into methodologies and perspective which provide new illumination of the world.[125]

It seems necessary in the study of white-collar crime to construct a solid substantive and theoretical structure that will house and nourish what we come to know about such behavior: the legal process outlining (or failing to outline) its dimensions, its ingredients, its perpetrators, its consequences, and the responses that it elicits. It is a heady challenge to engage in a subject that at its core tells us a great deal of importance about the society in which we live and, perhaps, about ourselves as well.

ENDNOTES

CHAPTER 1

1. W. H. Auden, "September 1, 1939," in *Another Time* (London: Faber & Faber, 1996), 103; Isiah Berlin, *The Proper Study of Mankind: An Anthology of Essays*, eds., Henry Hardy and Roger Hausheer (London: Chatto & Windus, 1997), 628.

2. John Kobler, *The Life and World of Al Capone* (Greenwich, CT: Fawcett Crest, 1971), pp. 283, 313.

3. Edwin H. Sutherland, "White-Collar Criminality." *American Sociological Review*, 5 (1940), p. 3.

4. David Jones, *History of Criminology: A Philosophical Perspective* (New York: Greenwood Press, 1986), pp. 171–172.

5. Matthew Josephson, *The Robber Barons* (New York: Harcourt, Brace, 1934).

6. Sutherland, "White-Collar Criminality," p. 2.

7. Quoted in John Brooks, *Once in Golcanda: A True Drama of Wall Street, 1930–1938* (New York: Harper Colophon, 1969), p. 49.

8. Sutherland, "White Collar Criminality," p. 1.

9. Ibid., p. 2.

10. Alan Dershowitz, "Increasing Community Control Over Corporate Crime." *Yale Law Journal*, 71 (1961): 289–306.

11. Ken Auletrta, "The Howell Doctrine." In *Backstory: Inside the Business of News* (New York: Penguin, 2003), pp. 1–62.

12. Paul Jesilow, Henry N. Pontell, and Gilbert Geis, *Prescription for Profit: How Doctors Defraud Medicaid* (Berkeley: University of California Press, 1993).

13. Sutherland, "White-Collar Criminality," p. 4.

14. US Senate, Special Committee on the Investigation of the Munitions Industry [The Nye Report]. 74th Cong., 2d Sess., 1936, pp. 3–13.

15. Sutherland, "White-Collar Criminality," p. 4. The source is John T Flynn, *Graft in Business* (New York: Vantage Press, 1931), p. 55.

16. Walter Lippmann, "The Themes of Muckraking." In *Drift and Mastery: An Attempt to Diagnose the Current Unrest* (Englewood Cliffs, NJ: Prentice-Hall, 1961), p. 30.

17. See *United States v. Manton*, 107 F.2d 834 (2nd Cir. 1938), *cert. denied*, 309 U.S. 664 (1940).

18. See Lawrence H. Larsen and Nancy J. Hulston, *Pendergast* (Columbia: University of Missouri Press, 1997). Pendergast received a 15-month prison

sentence. The bribe was to be used to pay off gambling debts. Pendergast is best remembered today as the man who selected Harrry S. Truman, now one of the most highly respected American presidents, to run for the US Senate. In 1926, Kansas City, Missouri, run by Pendergast, was regarded as the wildest city in America, "filled with bars, brothels, and gambling dens in which, one reporter wrote, 'the operators doctor the dice in such a manner as to make a loss to them a gravitational impossibility.'" Yet Pendergast himself was an abstentious, churchgoing family man who was in bed every night at nine. Geoffrey C. Ward, *Jazz: A History of America's Music* (New York: Alfred A. Knopf, 2000), p. 196.

19. Sutherland, "White Collar Criminality," p. 7.

20. John T. Noonan, Jr., and Dan M. Kahan, "Bribery." In Joshua Dressler, ed. *Encyclopedia of Crime & Justice*, 2nd ed. (New York: Macmillan Reference, 2002), p. 110a.

21. *United States v. Myers,* 692 F.2d 832 (2nd Cir. 1982), *cert. denied*, 461 U.S. 961 (1983).

22. See United States Congress. House of Representatives, Committee on Standards of Official Conduct. "In the Matter of Representative James A. Trafficant, Jr." 107 Cong., 2nd Sess., 2002.

23. Ibid., pp. 8–9. The source is Bouck White, *The Book of Daniel Drew: A Glimpse of the Fisk-Gould-Tweed Régime from the Inside* (Larchmont, NY: American Research Council, 1965), p. 268.

24. W. J. Millor and Christopher N. L. Brooke, eds., "To Bartolomew, Bishop of Essex" [Letter 174], *The Letters of John of Salisbury* (Oxford: Clarendon Press, 1979), Vol. II, pp. 149, 151. See also John T. Noonan, Jr., *Bribes* (New York: Macmillan, 1984), p. 165.

25. Valerius Maximus, *Memorable Writings and Sayings*. D. R. Shackleton Bailey, ed. & trans. (Cambridge, MA: Harvard University Press, 2000), Vol. II.2, ext.14, pp. 123, 125.

26. Jan Frederick Kindstrand, *Anarcharsis: The Legend and the Apophthegma* (Stockholm: Almquist & Wicksell, 1981), pp. 149–150.

27. Jonathan Swift, "An Essay Upon the Faculties of the Mind." In *The Works of Dean Swift*. (New York: Derby & Jackson, 1857), p. 291.

28. John Adams, "Ancient Democratic Republics: Athens [Letter XLI]. In *A Defence of the Constitutions of the Government of the United States of America* (London: C. Dilly, 1787), Vol. I, p. 283.

29. Sutherland, "White Collar Criminality," pp. 4–5.

30. Edwin H. Sutherland, "Crimes of Corporations." In Albert Cohen, Alfred Lindesmith, and Karl Schuessler, eds. *The Sutherland Papers* (Bloomington: Indiana University Press, 1956), p. 96.

31. Edwin H. Sutherland, "The Sexual Psychopath Laws." *Journal of Criminal Law and Criminology*, 40 (1950), p. 554. See also John F. Galliher and Cheryl Tyree, "Edwin Sutherland's Research on the Origins of Sexual Psychopath

Laws: An Early Case Study of the Medicalization of Deviance." *Social Problems,* 33 (1985), pp. 100–113.

32. Thomas Szasz, *Law, Liberty, and Psychiatry: An Inquiry into the Social Uses of Mental Health Practices* (New York: Macmillan, 1963), p. 23.

33. Sutherland, "White Collar Criminality," p. 9.

34. Michael R. Gottfredson and Travis Hirschi, *A General Theory of Crime* (Stanford, CA: Stanford University Press, 1990).

35. Sutherland, "White Collar Criminality," pp. 10–11.

36. Edwin H. Sutherland, "Social Process in Behavior Problems." *Publications of the American Sociological Society,* 26 (1932): 59–60.

37. Edwin H. Sutherland and Harvey J. Locke, *Twenty Thousand Homeless Men: A Study of Unemployed Men in Chicago Shelters* (Philadelphia: Lippincott, 1936), p. 62.

38. Edwin H. Sutherland, *Principles of Criminology,* 2nd ed. (Philadelphia: Lippincott, 1934), p. 32.

39. Edward A. Ross, "The Criminaloid," *Atlantic Monthly,* 99 (1907), p. 46. Ross expands on these ideas in *Sin and Society: An Analysis of Latter Day Iniquity* (Boston: Houghton Mifflin, 1907).

40. Edward A. Ross, *Seventy Years of It: An Autobiography* (New York: D. Appleton-Century, 1936), p. 180.

41. Sutherland to Luther Bernard, November 19, 1916. Bernard papers, Pattee Library, Pennsylvania State University, University Park, PA.

42. Warren J. Samuels, "The Firing of E. A. Ross from Stanford University: Injustice Compounded by Deception?" *Journal of Economic Education,* 22 (1990): 183–190; James C. Mohr, "Academic Turmoil and Public Opinion: The Ross Case at Stanford." *Pacific Historical Review,* 39 (1970): 39–61. See generally Sean N. McMahon, *Social Control and the Public Interest: The Legacy of Edward A. Ross* (New Brunswick, NJ: Transaction, 1999). Ross appeared at a reception for graduate students in 1949 during my first year at the University of Wisconsin. He was a huge man. Though he was sitting in a wheelchair, I had the impression he still was taller than anybody there. He was disliked by the Wisconsin sociology faculty of the time; they considered him unpleasantly imperious.

43. White, *Daniel Drew,* p. 128.

44. Edward. A. Ross, *Seventy Years of It.*

45. "Poverty Belittled as Crime Factor," *Philadelphia Public Ledger.* December 28, 1939, p. 17.

46. "Hits Criminality in White Collars," *New York Times.* December 28, 1939, p. 1.

47. Leon Bramson, *The Political Context of Sociology.* Cambridge, MA: Harvard University Press, 1961, pp. 93–94.

48. Robert Jay Lifton, *The Nazi Doctors: Medical Killing and the Psychology of Genocide* (New York: Basic Books, 1984), p. 14.

49. Janet Malcolm, "The Silent Woman." *The New Yorker*, August 23 and 30, 1993, p. 148.

50. Sutherland, "White-Collar Criminality," p. 1.

51. Edwin H. Sutherland, *White Collar Crime* (New York: Dryden, 1949), p. v. All later references are to this edition.

52. Edwin H. Sutherland, *White Collar Crime: The Uncut Version* (New Haven, CT: Yale University Press), 1983.

53. Somewhat inspired by Sutherland, this was this subject of my first venture into research on white-collar crime: Gilbert Geis, "The NAM in the Schools." *The Progressive* 14 (May 1950): 11–12.

54. Sutherland, *White Collar Crime*, p. 210.

55. See, e.g., Howard Odum, "Edwin H. Sutherland (1883–1950)." *Social Forces*, 29 (1951), p. 348.

56. Jerome Hall, "Edwin H. Sutherland (1883–1950). *Journal of Criminal Law and Criminology*, 41 (1950), p. 394.

57. Edwin Sutherland to Todd Stoops, November 11, 1942.

58. Todd Stoops. Letter to Edwin H. Sutherland, November 15, 1942.

59. Sutherland. Letter to Stoops, November 16, 1942.

60. Jon Huer, *The Wages of Sin: America's Dilemma of Profit Against Humanity* (New York: Praeger, 1991), pp. 228–229.

61. Margaret James, *Social Problems and Policies during the Puritan Revolution, 1640–1660* (New York: Barnes & Noble, 1966), p. 326.

62. Anatole France, *Le Lys Rouge* [The Red Ruby]. Paris: Calmann-Lévy, 1894, p. 117.

63. George Bernard Shaw, *The Crime of Imprisonment* (New York: Philosophical Library, 1946), pp. 69–70.

64. Harvey Katz, "The White Collar Criminal." *Washingtonian* (May 1970), p. 65.

65. J. Kelly Strader, "Judicial Politics of White Collar Crime." *Hastings Law Journal*, 50 (1999), p. 1268.

66. *United States v. Kohlback*, 38 F.3d 832, 838 (6th Cir. 1994).

67. *United States v. McClatchey*, 316 F.3d 1122, 1135 (10th Cir. 2003).

68. Richard M. Cohen and Jules Witcover, *A Heartbeat Away: The Investigation and Prosecution of Spiro T. Agnew* (New York: Viking, 1971), p. 71.

69. Paul W. Tappan, "Who is the Criminal?" *American Sociological Review*, 12 (1947): 96–102. See also Robert G. Caldwell, "A Re-Examination of the Concept of White-Collar Crime." *Federal Probation*, 22 (March 1958): 30–36.

70. Jerome Hall, "Theft, White Collar Crime and the Corporation: The Need for a National Institute of Criminal Law and Criminology." In *Law, Social Science and Criminal Theory* (Littleton, CO: Fred B. Rothman, 1982), p. 277. My copy of *White Collar Crime* has Hall's Ex Libris and the dedication "With compliments of the author, Edwin." Colin Goff persuaded Hall, who was on the verge of donating the book to the Hastings Law School library, to exchange this copy for my unsigned one.

71. Sutherland, *White Collar Crime*, p. 13.

72. OED, 2d ed., vol. 20, p. 275. The dictionary traces the term to an alleged 1932 article by Sutherland which it identifies as "The Financial Crimes of the White Collar Class." Sutherland never wrote such an article.

73. Lonnie Athens, *The Creation of Dangerous Violent Criminals* (Urbana: University of Illinois Press, 1987), p. 111.

74. Ibid., p. 237. For a collection of more recent similar stories supplied by students, see Paul Blumberg, *The Predatory Society: Deception in the American Marketplace* (New York: Oxford University Press, 1989).

75. Hermann Mannheim, "White Collar Crime." *Annals of the American Academy of Political and Social Science*, 226 (1949), p. 244.

76. Selden D. Bacon, "White Collar Crime." *American Sociological Review*, 15 (1950), p. 309.

77. Jerome Michael and Mortimer J. Adler, *Crime, Law and Social Science* (New York: Harcourt, Brace, 1933).

78. Robert C. Sorenson, "White Collar Crime." *Harvard Law Review*, 41 (1950), p. 80.

79. Thomas I. Emerson, "White Collar Crime." *Yale Law Journal*, 59 (196): 583–585.

80. An excellent comprehensive study of Sutherland's background is Colin Goff, *Edwin H. Sutherland and White-Collar Crime*. Ph.D. dissertation, University of California, Irvine, 1983. I am greatly indebted to Goff's research in many parts of this chapter.

81. George Sutherland, *Reminisces* (Rochester, NY: American Baptist Historical Society, 1935), p. 149.

82. Roger Lane, *Murder in America: A History* (Columbus: Ohio State University Press, 1997), p. 174.

83. Donald R. Cressey, Letter to the author, February 10, 1981.

84. Robert W. Cherney, *Populism, Progressivism, and the Transformation of Nebraska Politics, 1885–1915* (Lincoln: University of Nebraska Press, 1981), p. xv.

85. John D. Hicks, *The Populist Revolt: A History of the Farmer's Alliance and the People's Party* (Lincoln: University of Nebraska Press, 1961), p. 291.

86. Cherney, *Populism*, p. 41.

87. Norman Pollack, *The Human Economy: Populism, Capitalism, and Democracy* (New Brunswick, NJ: Rutgers University Press, 1990), pp. 1, 167.

88. David B. Danhorn, *The World of Hope: Progressives and the Struggle for an Ethical Public Life* (Philadelphia: Temple University Press, 1987), p. 95.

89. Ruth Kornhauser, *Social Sources of Delinquency: An Appraisal of Analytic Models*. (Chicago: University of Chicago Press, 1978), p. 203.

90. Cesare Lombroso, *Crime: Its Causes and Remedies*, trans. by Henry P. Horton (Boston: Little, Brown, 1918), p. xxxv.

91. Ibid., pp. 44–45.

92. Ibid., pp. 374–375.

93. Charles R. Henderson, "Business Men and Social Theorists," *American Journal of Sociology*, 1 (1896): 389–390.

94. Cecil E. Greek, *The Religious Roots of Academic Sociology* (New York: Garland, 1992), p. 127.

95. Charles R. Henderson, *Introduction to the Study of Dependent, Defective, and Delinquent Children.* 2nd ed. (Boston, MA: Heath, 1901), p. 250.

96. Edwin H. Sutherland , Letter to Luther Bernard, July 13, 1927. Bernard papers, Pattee Library, Pennsylvania State University, University Park, PA.

97. Ibid., May 17, 1913.

98. Albion W. Small, "The State and Semi-Public Corporations." *American Journal of Sociology*, 1 (1890), pp. 403, 405, 408.

99. Thorstein Veblen, *The Theory of the Leisure Class* (New York: Macmillan, 1912), p. 237. See generally Michael Spindler, *Veblen and Modern America: Revolutionary Iconoclast* (London: Pluto Press).

100. Sutherland to Bernard, July 13, 1927.

101. Robert Franklin Hoxie, *Trade Unionism in the United States*, 2d ed. (New York: D. Appleton, 1923), p. 271.

102. Ibid., p. 386.

103. Edwin H. Sutherland, *Criminology* (Philadelphia: Lippincott, 1924), p. 621.

104. Albert Morris, *Criminology* (New York: Longmans Green, 1935), p. 153.

105. Kenneth Neill Cameron, *Stalin, a Man of Contradictions* (Toronto: NC Press, 1987).

106. Albert K. Cohen, "Mary Bess Cameron (1915–1988)." *Footnotes* (September–October 1998), p. 15.

107. Mary Owen Cameron. Interview with the author, October 27, 1992; see also "Mary Bess Owen Cameron." In Judith Porter Adams, ed. *Peacework: Oral Histories of Women Peace Activists* (New York: Twayne, 1990), pp. 94–99. Ms. Cameron's opinion of Sutherland's caution in the face of possible controversy was seconded by Albert K. Cohen, a younger colleague of Sutherland at Indiana. Cohen and Alfred Lindesmith, another Indiana sociology professor, had approached Sutherland, the department chair, advocating the appointment of Ray Oakley, an African American, as a teaching assistant. "Sutherland truly was color-blind," said Cohen, who admired him greatly, but his response to what at the time would have been a very controversial move was: "What are you, some kind of do-gooders?" Albert K. Cohen, interview with the author, August 23, 1980. To his considerable credit Sutherland was outspoken in his condemnation of the recent internment of 120,000 Japanese, many of them American citizens, in "relocation centers" in an interview printed in the student newspaper of the University of Washington, where he was teaching summer school. He said that the government was acting more in terms of "race prejudice than military necessity." "Campus Impresses Sutherland," *The Daily*, August 6, 1942, p. 1.

108. Mary Owen Cameron, *The Booster and the Snitch: Department Store Shoplifting* (New York: Free Press, 1964).

109. Lois Howard, telephone interview, June 26, 1993.

110. Donald Clemmer, *The Prison Community* (New York: Rinehart, 1958).

111. Donald Clemmer. Letter to Ben Reitman, September 23, 1950. Courtesy of the University of Illinois at Chicago Library.

112. Roger A. Bruns, *The Damndest Radical: The Life and World of Ben Reitman, Chicago's Celebrated Social Reformer, Hobo King, and Whorehouse Physician* (Urbana: University of Illinois Press, 1987); Marcia Reitman, *No Regrets: Ben Reitman and the Women Who Loved Him* (Lexington, MA: SouthSide Press, 1999). On Emma Goldman see her *Living My Life* (Garden City, NY: Garden City Publishing Co., 1933); Alice Wexler, *Emma Goldman: An Intimate Life* (New York: Pantheon, 1984).

113. Ernest D. MacDougall, ed., *Crime for Profit: A Symposium on Mercenary Crime* (Boston: Stratford, 1933).

114. Ovid Demaris, *The Director: An Oral Biography of J. Edgar Hoover* (New York: Harper's Magazine Press, 1975), p. 77.

115. Edwin H. Sutherland, "Parole in Indiana." *News Bulletin of the Osborne Association*, 9 (February 1938), pp. 1–2.

116. Gilbert Geis and Colin Goff, "Lifting the Cover from Undercover Operations: J. Edgar Hoover and Some of the Other Criminologists." *Crime, Law and Social Change*, 18 (1992): 91–104.

117. Leonard Orland, "Reflections on Corporate Crime: Law in Search of Theory and Scholarship." *American Criminal Law Review*, 17 (1980), p. 505. In 2004, law professor John S. Baker, Jr. took something of the same line as Orland. He offered the rather off-the-wall observation that the idea of white-collar crime had "created stigma and presumption of guilt among alleged corporate criminals" and that "the war on terrorism and organized crime may implicitly place corporate criminals in the same category as mobsters and terrorists." To this he added, rather gratuitously: "Although Marxist academics might wish it were so, it is not a crime to be wealthy or powerful." John S. Baker, Jr., "Reforming Corporations Through Threat of Federal Prosecution." *Cornell Law Review*, 80 (2004), pp. 313, 343, 344. Sutherland, hardly a Marxist, would not have disagreed with this last point: rather, he would have said that it is a crime to behave criminally, whether or not you are wealthy and powerful.

118. Edwin H. Sutherland, "A & P Propaganda, and Free Enterprise." Unpublished paper in possession of Karl Schuessler, Department of Sociology, Indiana University.

119. William I. Walsh, *The Rise and Decline of the Great Atlantic & Pacific Tea Company* (Secaucus, NJ: Lyle Stuart, 1986).

120. Leon S. Sheleff, *Ultimate Penalties: Capital Punishment, Life Imprisonment, Physical Torture* (Columbus: Ohio State University Press, 1987).

121. Marvin E. Wolfgang, Robert M. Figlio, and Terence P. Thornberry, *Examining Criminology* (New York: Elsevier, 1978).

122. Edwin H. Sutherland, *El Delito de Cuello Blanco*, Rosa del Olmo, trans. (Caracas: Universidad Central de Venezuela, Ediciones de la Biblioteca, 1969); Sutherland, *White Collar Crime*, Ryuchi Hirano and Kōji Iguchi, trans. (Tokyo: Iwanami Shoten, 1955); Sutherland, *Il Crimine dei Colletti Bianchi*, Gabrio Forti, trans. (Milan: Dott, A. Giuffre Editore, 1987).

123. Hermann Mannheim, *Comparative Criminology* (London: Routledge & Kegan Paul 1987), Vol. II, p. 470.

CHAPTER 2

1. James Q. Wilson, *The Moral Sense* (New York: Free Press, 1993), pp. 1–2. Wilson indicates that he deliberately uses "men" throughout his book because from time immemorial it has referred to any person whose gender was not specified and because he finds today's gender-based circumlocutions "awkward" and "wooden." Ibid., p. viii.

2. Warren E. Buffett, *Berkshire-Hathaway, Inc.: Annual Report* (Omaha, NE, 2002), p. 16.

3. Thurston Clarke, *California Fault: Searching for the Spirit of State Along the San Andreas* (New York: Ballantine, 1996), p. 104.

4. *Regina v. Jones*, 2 Lord Raymond 1013 (1703).

5. Cited in Stephen Schafer, *Theories in Criminology: Past and Present Philosophies of the Crime Problem* (New York: Random House, 1969), p. 77.

6. Stuart P. Green, "Moral Ambiguity in White Collar Criminal Law." *Notre Dame Journal of Law, Ethics & Public Policy*, 18 (2004), pp. 502, 513.

7. Robert F. Meier and Gilbert Geis, *Criminal Justice and Moral Issues: Prostitution, Narcotics, Homosexuality, Abortion, Pornography, and Gambling* (Los Angeles: Roxbury, 2006).

8. Stephen J. Carter, *God's Name in Vain: The Wrongs and Rights of Religion in Politics* (New York: Basic Books, 2000).

9. Plutarch, "Solon." In *The Rise and Fall of Athens: Nine Greek Lives*, Ian Scott-Kilvert, trans. (Baltimore: Penguin, 1960), p. 45.

10. Peter Garnsey, *Famine and Food Supply in the Greco-Roman World: Responses to Risk and Crisis* (Cambridge: Cambridge University Press, 1986), p. 76.

11. Phillip V. Stanley, *Ancient Greek Market Regulations and Control*. Ph.D. dissertation, University of California, Berkeley, 1976, p. 89.

12. Ray D. Henson, ed., *Landmarks of Law* (New York: Harper, 1960), p. xi.

13. Lysias, "Against the Retailers of Grain." In *Lysias*, Spencer C. Todd, trans. (Austin: University of Texas Press, 2000), p. 243.

14. Flavius Philostratus, *Philostratus in Honour of Appolonius of Tyana*, Frrederick. C. Conybeare, ed. (Cambridge, MA: Harvard University Press, 1912), p. 43.

15. William Wyatt Davenport, *Athens* (Amsterdam: Time-Life Books, 1978), 50.

16. William Illingworth, *An Inquiry into the Laws, Ancient and Modern, Regarding Forestalling, Regrating and Ingrossing* (London: E. and R. Brooke, 1800), p. 3.

17. Quoted in Lionel Trilling, *Matthew Arnold* (New York: Columbia University Press, 1949), p. 55.

18. Herbert C. Kelman and V. Lee Hamilton, *Crimes of Obedience: Toward a Social Psychology of Authority and Responsibility* (New Haven, CT.: Yale University Press, 1989), 62.

19. Quoted in Barbara W. Tuchman, *A Distant Mirror: The Calamitous 14th Century* (New York: Knopf, 1978), p. 37.

20. Pope Pius XI, *Quadragesimo Anno* [After Forty Years]. Paragraph 32 (1931). See also William Quigley, "Catholic Social Thought and the Amorality of Large Corporations: Time to Abolish Corporate Personhood." *Loyola Journal of Public Interest Law*, 5 (2004): 109–134.

21. Hershey H. Friedman, "Talmudic Business Ethics: An Historical Perspective." *Akron Business and Economic Review* (Winter 1980), p. 47.

22. Ibid., p. 49.

23. Edward Zipperstein, *Business Ethics in Jewish Law* (New York: KTAV Publishing House, 1983), p. 73.

24. Max May, "Jewish Criminal Law and Legal Procedure." *Journal of Criminal Law*, 31 (1940): 438–447.

25. Gustave de Beaumont and Alexis de Tocqueville, *On the Penitentiary System in the United States and its Application to France*, Francis Lieber, trans. (Carbondale: Southern Illinois University Press, 1964).

26. John Noonan, Jr., *Bribes* (New York: Macmillan, 1984), p. 248.

27. Dante Alighieri, *Inferno*, Charles S. Singleton, trans. (London: Routledge & Kegan Paul, 1970), Canto XI, lines 25–28, p. 111; see also Paul G. Chevigny, "From Betrayal to Violence: Dante's *Inferno* and the Social Construction of Crime." *Law & Social Inquiry*, 25 (2001): 787–818.

28. Tuchman, *A Distinct Mirror*, p. 576.

29. Marcus Tullius Cicero, *De Officiis*, Walter Miller, trans. (Cambridge, MA: Harvard University Press, 1913), Book III, xi–xiii.

30. Thomas Aquinas, *Summa Theologica* (New York: McGraw-Hill, 1969), 11KK, qv.77.9.3, ch. 3.

31. Thomas Donaldson, *Corporations and Morality* (Englewood Cliffs, NJ: Prentice-Hall, 1982).

32. Ian Breward, ed., *The Works of William Perkins* (Abington, Berks.: Courtenay Press, 1970).

33. John Bunyan, *The Life and Death of Mr. Badman*, James F. Forrest and Roger Shattuck, eds. (Oxford: Clarendon Press, 1985), pp. 108–110.

34. Charles Sommerville, *The Discovery of Childhood in Puritan England* (Athens: University of George Press, 1992), pp. 140–141.

35. Thomas Hobbes, "Leviathan." In *Works of Thomas Hobbes of Malmesbury*, William Molesworth, ed. (London: J. Bohn, 1839–1845), Vol. III, p. 321.

36. James A. Sharpe, *Crime in Seventeenth Century England: A County Study* (Cambridge: Cambridge University Press, 1983), p. 39.

37. Daniel Defore, *Complete English Tradesman, in Familiar Letters, Directing Him in All the Several Parts and Progressions of Trade* (New York: A.M. Kelly, 1969), p. 189.

38. Christopher Hill, *Society and Puritanism in Pre-Revolutionary England* (London: Secker & Warburg, 1964), 33.

39. Edward Bellamy, *Looking Backward, 2000–1887* (Boston: Houghton Mifflin, 1926).

40. Clive S. Lewis, *The Screwtape Letters; Screwtape Proposes a Toast*, Rev. ed. (New York: Macmillan, 1982), p. 6.

41. Quoted in Tim Hilton, *John Ruskin: The Later Years* (New Haven, CT: Yale University Press, 2000), p. 332.

42. The word does not appear in *The Oxford English Dictionary*. I e-mailed the OED editors asking for a definition. They acknowledged the request, and said that they would look into the matter, but two years later they have not let me know the word's definition. It apparently refers to some kind of official of the time.

43. Illingworth, *An Inquiry into the Laws*, p. 4.

44. Richard Epstein, "History Lean: The Reconciliation of Private Property and Representative Government." *Columbia Law Review*, 95 (1995), p. 600.

45. Quoted in Illingworth, *An Inquiry into the Laws*, p. 5.

46. 31 Edward I, Statute 5 (1306).

47. Alan Everitt, *Change in the Provinces: The Seventeenth Century* (Leicester, UK: Leicester University Press, 1969), p. 39.

48. Quoted in Andrew B. Appleby, *Famine in Tudor and Stuart England* (Stanford, CA: Stanford University Press, 1978), p. 143.

49. Joseph J. Ellis, *His Excellency George Washington* (New York: Alfred Knopf, 2004), p. 125.

50. Donald G. Barnes, *A History of English Corns Laws, from 1660 to 1846* (London: G. Routledge, 1930), pp. 81–82.

51. See, e.g., Gilbert Geis and Ivan Bunn, *A Trial of Witches: A Seventeenth-Century Witchcraft Prosecution* (London: Routledge, 1997).

52. Adam Smith, *An Inquiry into the Natural Causes of the Wealth of Nations*, Edwin Cannon, ed. (New York: Modern Library, 1994), pp. 490–491, 493.

53. Jeremy Bentham, *Jeremy Bentham's Economic Writings*, Werner, ed. (London: Allen & Unwin, 1952–1954), Vol. III, pp. 257–258.

54. Edmond Burke, "Thoughts and Detail on Scarcity Originally Presented to Right Hon. William Pitt in the Month of November 1790." In *The Works of the Right Honourable Edmund Burke* (London: F. & C. Riverton, 1803–1827), Vol. V, p. 150.

55. *Congressional Record*, 21 (1890), p. 3153.

56. *Standard Oil Co. v. United States*, 221 U.S. 1, 55 (1911).

57. Luke Owen Pike, *A History of Crime in England, Illustrating the Changes of the Laws in the Process of Civilisation* (London: Smith & Elder, 1873), Vol. II, pp. 101–102.

58. Hans Thorelli, *The Federal Antitrust Policy: Origination of an American Tradition* (Baltimore: Johns Hopkins Press, 1935), p. 151.

59. Louis Filler, *The Muckrakers* (University Park: The Pennsylvania State University Press, 1975), p. 330.

60. Roger Sharrock, *John Bunyan* (London: Hutchinson's University Library, 1954), p. 26.

61. William H. Harding, *John Bunyan: Pilgrim and Dreamer* (New York: F. Revell, 1928), see also Robert Adger Law, "Muck-Rackers before Bunyan," *Modern Language Notes 6* (1942): 455–457.

62. Isaac F. Marcosson, *David Graham Phillips and His Times* (New York: Dodd, Mead, 1932), pp. 238–241.

63. Theodore Roosevelt, "The Man with the Muckrake." In *The Works of Theodore Roosevelt* (New York: Scribner's, 1926), p. 416.

64. Albert B. Hart and Herbert R. Ferlager, *Theodore Roosevelt Cyclopedia*, Rev. ed. (Oyster Bay, NY: Theodore Roosevelt Association, 1989), p. 357.

65. Thomas W. Lawson, "Frenzied Finance." *Everybody's Magazine,* 12 (1905), pp. 173–174.

66. Ida M. Tarbell, *The History of the Standard Oil Company* (New York: Macmillan, 1939); Alice M. Fleming, *Ida Tarbell: First of the Muckrakers* (New York: Cromwell, 1971).

67. "Journalism's Greatest Hits," *New York Times* (March 1, 1999), p. C1.

68. *Standard Oil Company of New Jersey v. United States,* 221 U.S. 1, 30 (1911).

69. Ibid., p. 50.

70. 163 U.S. 537, 559 (1896). See also Thomas Brook, ed. *Plessy v. Ferguson: A Brief History with Documents* (Boston: Bedford Books, 1997).

71. Ibid., pp. 83–84.

72. Samuel S. McClure, "Editorial." *McClure's Magazine,* 22 (1903), pp. 344–345; see further Samuel S. McClure, *My Autobiography* (New York: Frederick A. Stokes, 1914).

73. Michael D. Marraccio, "Did a Business Conspiracy End Muckraking?" *Historian,* 47 (1985):, 58–71.

74. Cornelius C. Regier, *The Era of the Muckrakers* (Chapel Hill: University of North Carolina Press, 1932), p. 212.

75. Mary E. Tomkins, *Ida M. Tarbell* (New York: Twayne, 1974), p. 55.

76. Carl Bernstein and Bob Woodward, *All the President's Men* (New York: Simon & Schuster, 1974).

77. *Tavoulareas v. Piro,* 759 F. 2d. 90, 121 (D.C. District, 1985).

78. See Gabrio Forti and Marta Bertolino, eds., *La Televisione del Crimine* (Milan: Vita e Pensiero- Largo A. Gemelli), 2005.

79. Ralph Nader, "Business Crime." In David Sanford, ed. *Hot War on the Consumer* (New York: Putnam, 1969), p. 140.

CHAPTER 3

1. John C. Coffee, Jr., "'No Soul to Damn: No Body to Kick': An Unscandalized Inquiry into the Problem of Corporate Punishment." *Michigan Law Review,* 79 (1981): 386–459.

2. Henry Maine, *Ancient Law Its Connection with the Early History of Society and Its Relation to Modern Ideas,* 6th ed. (New York: Henry Holt).

3. Emanuel Celler, quoted in Anthony Sampson, *The Soverign State of ITT* (Greenwich, CT: Fawcett, 1973), p. 160.

4. Charles C. Abbott, *The Rise of the Business Corporation* (Ann Arbor, MI: Edwards Brothers, 1936), p. 2.

5. Ibid., p. 15.

6. Elizabeth Donnan, "The Early Days of the South Sea Company, 1711–1718." *Journal of Economic and Business History,* 2 (1930): 419–450.

7. William E. H. Lecky, *A History of England in the Eighteenth Century* (London: Longmans, 1907), Vol. I, p. 372.

8. Richard W. Boyden, *The English Business Corporation, 1660–1720.* Unpublished doctoral dissertation, Harvard University, 1948.

9. John Carswell, *The South Sea Bubble* (Stanford, CA: Stanford University Press, 1960), p. 10.

10. William R. Scott, *The Constitution and Finance of English, Scottish and Irish Joint-Stock Companies to 1720* (Cambridge: Cambridge University Press, 1910–1912), Vol. III, p. 297.

11. Ralph H. Mottram, *A History of Financial Speculation* (London: Chatto & Windus, 1929), p. 133.

12. 5 George I, c. 18 (1720). The term "bubble" derives from the dictionary definition of "a body of air that can easily burst."

13. Gerald R. Erleigh, *The South Sea Bubble* (New York: Putnam's, 1933), p. 95.

14. 4 George IV, c. 94 (1825).

15. Ron Harris, *Industrializing English Law: Entrepreneurship and Business Organization, 1720–1844* (Cambridge: Cambridge University Press, 2000); Armand B. DuBois, *The English Business Company After the Bubble Act, 1720–1800* (New York: Commonwealth Fund, 1938).

16. Virginia Cowles, *The Great Swindle: The Story of the South Sea Bubble* (New York: Harpers, 1960), p. 138.

17. Ibid., p. 160.

18. Carswell, p. 210; Erleigh, p. 128.

19. See Richard Dale, *The First Crash: Lessons from the South Sea Bubble* (Princeton, NJ: Princeton University Press, 2004); John Langdon-Davies, *The South Sea Bubble: A Collection of Contemporary Documents* (London: Cape, 1965).

20. *Dartmouth College v. Woodward,* 17 U.S. (4 Wheat.) 518, 636 (1819).

21. John W. Salmond, *Jurisprudence,* 6th ed. (London: Sweet and Maxwell, 1920), p. 285.

22. Phillip I. Blumberg, *The Multinational Challenge to Corporation Law: The Search for a New Corporate Personality* (New York: Oxford University Press, 1993), p. 6.

23. Glenn A. Clark, "Corporate Homicide: A New Assault on Corporate Decision-Making." *Notre Dame Law Review*, 54 (1979), p. 917.

24. Richard C. Litman and Donald S. Litman, "Reaction of the American Consumer: The Muckrakers and the Enforcement of the First Federal Food and Drug Law in the United States." *Federal Drug Cosmetic Law Journal*, 34 (1981), p. 650. For a similar view by Louis D. Brandeis, a highly regarded US Supreme Court judge, see *Louis K. Leggett Co. v. Lee*, 288 U.S. 517, 565 (1933).

25. David M. Chalmers, *Neither Socialism, Nor Monopoly: Theodore Roosevelt and the Decision to Regulate the Railroads* (Philadelphia: Lippincott, 1976), p. 1.

26. Robert L. Rubin, "Federal Regulation in Historical Perspective." *Stanford Law Review* 38 (1986), p. 1194.

27. Lawrence Friedman, *A History of American Law*, 2d ed. (New York: Simon and Schuster, 1985), p. 468.

28. *Santa Clara County v. Southern Pacific Railroad*, 18 U.S. 194 (1896).

29. *Hale v. Henkel*, 201 U.S. 43 (1986). See also Peter J. Henning, "The Conundrum of Corporate Criminal Liability: Seeking a Consistent Approach to the Constitutional Rights of Corporations in Criminal Prosecutions." *Tennessee Law Review*, 63 (1966): 792, 886.

30. Fon W. Boardman, Jr., *America and the Robber Barons* (New York: Henry Walck, 1977), p. 62.

31. Oscar Lewis, *The Big Four: The Story of Huntington, Stanford, Hopkins, and Crocker and the Building of the Central Pacific* (New York: Knopf, 1938), p. 11. See also David Haward, *Empire Express: Building the First Transcontinental Railroad* (New York: Viking, 2000).

32. *New York Central & Hudson River Railroad Co. v. United States*, 412 U.S. 481 (1908).

33. *Berea College v. Kentucky*, 211 U.S. 45 (1908).

34. Kathleen F. Brickey, "Rethinking Corporate Liability Under the Model Penal Code." *Rutgers Law Journal*, 9 (1988): 593–633.

35. Glanville Williams, *Proceedings of the 33rd Meeting of the American Law Institute* (Philadelphia: Institute, 1956), p. 159.

36. See Gilbert Geis and Joseph F. C. DiMento. "Empirical Evidence and the Doctrine of Corporate Criminal Liability." *American Journal of Criminal Law*, 29 (2002): 341–375.

37. Gerhard O. W. Mueller, "Mens Rea and the Corporation: A Study of the Model Penal Code Position on Corporate Criminal Liability." *University of Pittsburgh Law Review*, 19 (1957): 21–50.

38. American Law Institute, *Model Penal Code*. Tentative Draft No. 4 (Philadelphia: Institute, 1956), §2.07(4).

39. *United States v. Hilton Hotels Corp.*, 467 F.2d 1006 (9th Cir. 1972), *cert. denied*, 408 U.S. 1125 (1973).

40. *United States v. Bank of New England*, 821 F.2d 844, 875 (1st Cir. 1987), *cert denied*, 484 U.S. 843.

41. Laurie J. Rodriguez and David E. Barlow, "Structural Contradiction and the United States Sentencing Commission: The Development of Federal

Organizational Sentencing Guidelines." *Crime, Law and Social Change*, 32 (1999): 169–181.

42. United States Sentencing Commission, *Supplementary Report on Guidelines for Organizations* (Washington, DC: Government Printing Office, 1991); see also William S. Laufer, "Corporate Prosecution, Cooperation, and the Trading of Favors." *Iowa Law Review*, 87 (2002): 612–667; Donna E. Murphy, "The Federal Sentencing Guidelines for Organizations: A Decade of Monitoring Compliance and Ethics." *Iowa Law Review*, 87 (2002): 697–719.

43. Klaus-Dieter Benner, "Forms of Criminal Responsibility of Organizations and Reasons for Their Development." In Albin Esser, Gunter Heine, and Barbara Huber, eds., *Criminal Responsibility of Legal and Collective Entities* (Freiburg im Breisgau: Edition Juscrim, 1999), p. 57.

44. Robert A. Kagan and John T. Scholz, "The 'Criminology of the Corporation' and Regulatory Enforcement Strategies." In Keith Hawkins and John M. Thomas, eds., *Enforcing Regulation* (Boston: Kluwer, 1984).

45. Keith Hawkins, *Environment and Enforcement: Regulation and the Social Definition of Pollution* (Oxford: Clarendon, 1984).

46. Victor S. Khanna, "Corporate Criminal Liability: What Purpose Does It Serve?" *Harvard Law Review*, 109 (1996): 1477–1534.

47. David Barstow, "A Trench Caves In, a Young Worked Is Dead. Is It a Crime?" *New York Times*, December 21, 2003, p. 1.

48. Thomas R. Clay and Gilbert Geis, "Criminal Enforcement of California's Occupational Carcinogens Control Act. *Temple Law Quarterly*, 51 (1980): 1067–1099.

49. Barstow, "A Trench Caves In." 1.

50. Loren Fox, *Enron: The Rise and Fall* (Hoboken, NJ: John Wiley, 2003); Mimi Schwartz and Sharon Watkins, *Power Failure: The Inside Story of the Collapse of Enron* (New York: Doubleday, 2003).

51. Susan E. Squires, Cynthia Smith, Lorna McDougall, and William B. Yeack, *Inside Arthur Andersen: Shifting Values, Unexpected Consequences* (Upper Saddle River, NJ: Prentice Hall, 2003).

52. Barbara Ley Toffler and Jennifer Reingold, *Final Accounting: Ambition, Greed, and the Fall of Arthur Andersen* (New York: Broadway Books, 2003).

53. Joseph T. Wells, *Frankensteins of Fraud: The 20th Century's Top Ten White-Collar Criminals* (Austin, TX: Obsidian, 2000), pp. 23–70.

54. Quoted in Stuart P. Green, "Moral Ambiguity in White Collar Criminal Law." *Notre Dame Journal of Law, Ethics & Public Policy*, 18 (2004), p. 504.

55. Stephen N. Rosoff, Henry N. Pontell, and Robert Tillman, *Profit Without Honor: White Collar Crime and the Looting of America*, 3rd ed. (Upper Saddle River, NJ: Prentice Hall, 2004), p. 294.

56. Peter H. Schuck, *Agent Orange on Trial: Mass Toxic Disaster in the Courts* (Cambridge, MA: Belknap, 1987).

57. *Arthur Andersen LLP v. United States*, ___ U.S. ____; No. 04-368; 2005 Lexis 4348 (May 31, 2005).

58. Harry Glasbeck, *Wealth by Stealth: Corporate Crime, Corporate Law, and the Perversion of Democracy* (Toronto: Between the Lines, 2002).

59. James Surowiecki, "Sarboxed In?" *The New Yorker*, December 12, 2005, 46.

60. 15 United States Code §§7245-7256 (2002).

61. *Lampf v. Gilbertson*, 501 U.S. 111 (1991).

62. Tania Brief and Terrell McSweeney, "Corporate Criminal Liability." *American Criminal Law Review*, 40 (2002), p. 339.

63. Ethan G. Zelitzer, "The Sarbanes-Oxley Act: Accounting for Corporate Corruption?" *Loyola Consumer Law Review*, 15 (2002): 27–55.

64. *United States v. Scrushy*, CR-03-BE 0530-S (November 23, 2004).

65. Simon Romero and Kyle Whitmire, "Scrushy on Trial: Class, Race and the Pursuit of Justice in Alabama." *New York Times*, May 31, 2005, p. C8.

66. Chad Terhune and Dan Morse, "Why Scrushy Won His Trial and Ebbers Lost," *Wall Street Journal*, June 30, 2005, C1; Dan Morse, Chad Terhune, and Ann Carns, "HealthSouth's Scrushy is Acquitted," *Wall Street Journal*, June 29, 2005, A1, A8.

67. Pamela H. Bucy, *White-Collar Crime: Cases and Materials* (St. Paul, Minn.: West Group, 1998).

68. Reed Abelson and Jonathan Glater, "A Style that Connects with Hometown Jurors," *New York Times*, June 29, 2005, 4. For a hard-hitting critique of U.S. legal procedures, see WIlliam T. Pizzi, *Trial Without Truth: Why Our System of Criminal Trial Has Become an Expensive Failure and What We Need to do to Rebuild It* (New York: New York University Press, 1999).

69. Joseph F. C. DiMento, Gilbert Geis, and Julia Gelfand, "Corporate Criminal Liability: A Bibliography." *Western State University Law Review*, 28 (2001): 255–275.

70. Warren Buffett, *Berkshire-Hathaway, Inc.: 2002 Annual Report* (Omaha, NB: Berkshire-Hathaway, 2003), p. 16.

71. "The Boss's Pay," *Wall Street Journal*, April 12, 2004, p. B6.

72. Buffett, *Berkshire-Hathaway*, Ibid.

73. Ronald Alsop, "Corporate Scandal Hits Home." *Wall Street Journal*, February 10, 2004, p. B4.

74. Ian Ayres and John Braithwaite, *Responsive Regulation: Transcending the Deregulation Debate* (New York: Oxford University Press, 1992), p. 110.

75. Jonathan Wiseman, "IRS Speeds Corporate Tax Audits," *Washington Post*, December 23, 2001, A01

76. Jonathan Wiseman, "IRS Speeds Corporate Tax Audits. *Washington Post*, December 23, 2001, p. AO1.

77. Sally S. Simpson, *Corporate Crime, Law, and Social Control* (New York: Cambridge University Press, 2002), p. xi.

78. Stanton Wheeler, Kenneth Mann, and Austin Sarat, *Sitting in Judgement: The Sentencing of White-Collar Criminals* (New Haven, CT: Yale University Press, 1988).

79. Marshall B. Clinard and Peter C. Yeager, *Corporate Crime* (New York: Free Press, 1980).

80. Albert J. Reiss, Jr. and Albert Biderman, *Data Sources on White-Collar Crime Law-Breaking* (Washington, DC: US Department of Justice, 1980).

81. Leonard Orland, "Reflections on Corporate Crime: Law in Search of Theory and Scholarship." *American Criminal Law Review*, 17 (1980), p. 510.

82. For an excellent examination of the quality of the FBI reports see William J. Chambliss, "The Politics of Crime Statistics." In Colin Sumner, ed., *The Blackwell Companion to Criminology* (Malden, MA: Blackwell, 2004), pp. 452–470.

83. Eugene Szwaijkowski, "Organizational Illegality, Theoretical Integration and Illustrative Application." *Academy of Management Journal*, 10 (1985), p. 566.

84. Glenn Jacobs, ed., *The Participant-Observer* (New York: G. Braziller, 1970); William Foote Whyte, *Participant Observer: An Autobiography* (Ithaca, NY: ILR Press, 1994).

85. Diane Vaughan, *The Challenger Launch Decision: Risky Technology, Culture and Deviance at NASA* (Chicago: University of Chicago Press, 1996). See also Vaughan, "Rational Choice, Situated Action, and the Social Control of Organizations." *Law & Society Review*, 32 (1998), p. 23.

86. John C. Coffee, Jr., "Corporate Crime and Punishment: A Non-Chicago View of the Economics of Criminal Sanctions." *American Criminal Law Review*, 17 (1980), p. 462.

87. Leo G. Barille, "A Soul to Damn and a Body to Kick: Imprisoning Corporate Criminals." *Humanity and Society*, 17 (1993), p. 190.

88. See, for instance, Harry Kalven, Jr. Hans Zeisel, Thomas Callahan, and Phillip Ennis, *The American Jury* (Chicago: University of Chicago Press, 1971); Valerie P. Hans, *Business on Trial: Jury and Corporate Responsibility* (New Haven, CT: Yale University Press, 2000).

89. Stephen M. Rosoff, "Physicians as Criminal Defendants: Specialty, Sanctions, and Status Liability, *Law and Human Behavior*, 13 (1989): 231–235.

90. Brent Fisse and John Braithwaite, *The Impact of Publicity on Corporate Offenders* (Albany: State University of New York Press, 1983).

91. Albert W. Alschuler, "Ancient Law and the Punishment of Corporations: Of Frankpledge and Deodand." *Boston University Law Review*, 71 (1991): 311–312.

92. John Braithwaite and Brent Fisse, "Varieties of Responsibility and Organizational Crime." *Law and Policy*, 7 (1985), p. 325.

93. David O. Friedrichs, *Trusted Criminals: White Collar Crime and Accountability* (Belmont, CA: Wadsworth, 1996), p. 266.

94. Feliks M. Reshetnikov, "Criminal Liability of Corporations." In Hans de Doelder and Klaus Tiedemann, eds., *Le Criminalisation du Comportement Collectif: Criminal Liability of Corporations.* (Boston: Kluwer Law International, 1996), p. 343.

95. Kenneth Dau-Schmidt, "An Economic Analysis of the Criminal Law as Preference-Shaping Policy." *Duke Law Journal* (1990): 1–38.

96. Donald Black, *The Social Structure of Right and Wrong* (San Diego, CA: Academic Press, 1993), p. 55.
97. Coffee, "Corporate Crime," p. 463.
98. John C. Coffee, Jr., "Corporate Criminal Responsibility." In Sanford H. Kadish, ed., *Encyclopedia of Crime and Justice* (New York: Free Press, 1983), p. 260a.
99. Coffee, "No Soul to Damn," p. 387.
100. "Developments in the Law - Corporate Crime: Regulating Corporate Behavior Through Criminal Sanctions." *Harvard Law Review*, 92 (1978), p. 1367.
101. David von Ebers, "The Application of Criminal Homicide Statutes to Work-Related Death: Mens Rea and Deterrence." *Illinois Law Review*, (1986), p. 989.
102. Orland, "Reflections," p. 513.
103. Ibid., p. 503.
104. David Riesman, "Law and Sociology: Recruitment, Training, and Colleagueship." *Stanford Law Review*, 9 (1965), p. 651.
105. Louis D. Brandeis, "The Living Law." In Osmond K. Fraenkel, ed. *The Curse of Bigness* (New York: Viking Press, 1934), p. 325.
106. *Sweezey v. New Hampshire*, 354 U.S. 234, 261 (Frankfurter, J., dissenting).
107. Great Britain, *Report of the Committee on Local Authority and Allied Personal Services*. Command 3703 (1968), p. 45.

CHAPTER 4

1. Thorsten Sellin, *Culture Conflict and Crime* (New York: Social Science Research Council, 1938), pp. 20–21. See generally Peter J. Lejins, "Thorsten Sellin: A Life Dedicated to Criminology." *Criminology*, 27 (1987): 975–988.
2. Laureen Snider, "Traditional and Corporate Theft: A Comparison of Sanctions." In Peter Wickman and Timothy Dailey, eds. *White-Collar and Economic Crime: Multidisciplinary and Cross-National Perspectives* (Lexington, MA: Lexington Books, 1982), p. 237.
3. Edwin H. Sutherland, "White Collar Criminality." *American Sociological Review*, 5 (1940), p. 1.
4. Ibid.
5. Ibid., p. 4.
6. Ibid., p. 1.
7. Ibid., p. 2.
8. Alan Churchill, *The Incredible Ivar Kreuger* (London: Weidenfeld and Nicolson, 1967); Robert Shaplen, *Kreuger: Genius and Swindler* (New York: Knopf, 1980); Ulla Wallender, *Match Monopolies, 1925–1930*. Julie Sundquist, trans. (Stockholm: Liber, 1980).
9. Paul F. Jankowski, *Stavisky: A Confidence Man in the Republic of Virtue* (Ithaca, NY: Cornell University Press, 2002); Alexander Werth, *Framce in Turmoil* (Gloucester, MA: P. Smith, 1968). A 1974 motion picture, *Stavisky,*

starring Jean-Paul Belmondo is based on Stavisky's crooked dealings. The script has been published by Jorge Semprun and Alain Resnais, *Stavisky*, Sabine Desirée, trans. (New York: Viking, 1975).

10. Joseph T. Wells, "Citizen Coster: Philip Musica." In Wells, *Frankensteins of Fraud: The 20th Century's Top Ten White-Collar Criminals* (Austin, TX: Obsidian Publishing Company, 2002), p. 143. The present author worked during the summer of 1940 as what then was called an "office boy" at the McKesson & Robbins headquarters in downtown Manhattan, and remembers a room set aside to store the voluminous stacks of legal documents pertaining to the case against Musica-Coster.

11. Kitty Calavita and Henry N. Pontell, "'Other People's Money': Collective Embezzlement in the Savings and Loan and Insurance Industries." *Social Problems* 38 (1991): 94–112. See also Calavita, Pontell, and Robert H. Tillman, *Big Money Crime: Fraud and Politics in the Savings and Loan Crisis* (Berkeley: University of California Press, 1997); Stanton Wheeler and Mitchell L. Rothman, "The Organization as Weapon in White-Collar Crime." *Michigan Law Review*, 80 (1982): 1403–1436.

12. Marion D. Shutter, ed., *History of Minneapolis, Gateway to the Northwest* (Chicago: S. J. Clarke Publishing Co., 1923), Vol. II, pp. 454–457; "Foshay's Fall." *Time*, 11 (November 11, 1929), p. 54.

13. Ferdinand Pecora, *Wall Street Under Oath: The Story of Our Modern Money Changers* (New York: Simon and Schuster, 1939); John Brooks, *Once in Golconda: A True Drama of Wall Street, 1920–1938* (New York: W. W. Norton, 1969).

14. Morris R. Warner and Justin Starr, *Teapot Dome* (New York: Viking, 1959); David H. Stratton, *Tempest over Teapot Dome: The Story of Albert A. Fall* (Norman: University of Oklahoma Press, 1998).

15. Edwin H. Sutherland, *Principles of Criminology*, 3rd ed. (Philadelphia: Lippincott, 1939), pp. 36–37.

16. Ibid., p. 40.

17. Edwin H. Sutherland and Donald R. Cressey, *Principles of Criminology*, 5th ed. (Philadelphia: Lippincott, 1955), pp. 43–44.

18. Sutherland and Cressey, *Principles of Criinology*, 6th ed. (Philadelphia: Lippincott, 1960), p. 43.

19. Edwin H. Sutherland, "Is 'White-Collar Crime' Crime?" *American Sociological Review*, 10 (1945), p. 136.

20. Ibid. See further Gilbert Geis and Lawrence S. Salinger, "Antitrust and Organizational Deviance." In Peter A. Bamberger and William F. Sohnenstuhl, eds., *Research in the Sociology of Organizations* (Stamford, CT: JAI Press, 1998), pp. 71–110.

21. Kurt Eichenwald, *The Informant: A True Story* (New York: Broadway Books, 2000), p. 143.

22. Sutherland, "Is 'White-Collar Crime' Crime?" p. 138.

23. Steve Blum-West and Timothy J. Carter, "Bring White-Collar Crimes Back In: An Examination of Crimes and Torts." *Social Problems*, 30 (1972): 545–554.

24. Edwin H. Sutherland, "Crimes of Corporations." In Albert Cohen, Alfred Lindesmith, and Karl Schuessler, eds. *The Sutherland Papers* (Bloomington, IN: Indiana University Press, 1956), p. 79.

25. Alfred P. Sloan and Boyden Sparkes, *Adventures of a White Collar Man* (New York: Doubleday Doran, 1941).

26. "Alfred Pritchard Sloan, Jr." *Current Biography* (1940), p. 734.

27. Edwin H. Sutherland, *White Collar Crime* (New York: Dryden, 1949), p. 9.

28. Ibid.

29. Ibid.

30. Edwin H. Sutherland, *White Collar Crime: The Uncut Version* (New Haven, CT: Yale University Press, 1983), pp. 25–44.

31. Donald R. Cressey, "Poverty of Theory in Corporate Crime Research." *Advances in Criminological Theory*, 1 (1988): 31–56.

32. Edwin H. Sutherland, "The White Collar Criminal." In Vernon C. Branham and Samuel B. Kutash, eds. *Encyclopedia of Criminology* (New York: Philosophical Library, 1949), p. 511.

33. Ibid.

34. *Chiarella v. United States*, 445 U.S. 222 (1980); see also Elizabeth Szockyj, *The Law and Insider Trading: In Search of a Level Playing Field* (Buffalo, NY: William S. Hein, 1993).

35. Edwin Lemert, *Human Deviance, Social Problems, and Social Control*, 2nd ed. (Englewood Cliffs, NJ: Prentice-Hall, 1972), pp. 43–44; Jay Albanese, *White Collar Crime in America* (Englewood Cliffs, NJ: Prentice Hall, 1995), p. 2.

36. C. Wright Mills, *The Power Elite* (New York: Oxford University Press, 1956), pp. 343–344.

37. Albert J. Reiss, Jr., and Albert D. Biderrman. *Data Sources on White-Collar Lawbreaking* (Washington, DC: Government Printing Office, 1980), p. 4

38. John Braithwaite, "White Collar Crime." In Ralph H. Turner and James F. Short, Jr., eds., *Annual Review of Sociology* (Palo Alto, CA: Annual Reviews, 1985), Vol. 11, p. 3.

39. Frank E. Hartung, "White-Collar Offenses in the Wholesale Meat Industry in Detroit," *American Journal of Sociology*, 56 (1950), p. 25.

40. Ernest W. Burgess, "Comment, and Concluding Comment." *American Journal of Sociology*, 56 (1950): 31–34.

41. Paul W. Tappan, "Who Is the Criminal?" *American Sociological Review*, 12 (1947), p. 99.

42. Ibid, p. 98. A personal note regarding Tappan: I want to acknowledge his kindness to me when, early in my career, I pestered him with questions and with requests for job-hunting information. The last time I saw him was when we were on a panel together in Portland, Oregon. The Multnomah County sheriff's

department used his textbook in their training course and a squad car came by to take him to the airport. He invited me to go along, and off we went, sirens screaming. Earlier that evening, presumptuously, I have ventured to suggest that he was smoking too much. He took it good-naturedly. "It's too late now," he said. It was not very long afterward that he died of lung cancer. He was fifty-three years old.

43. The quoted material is from Colin H. Goff, *Edwin H. Sutherland and White-Collar Crime*. Ph.D. dissertation, University of California, 1982, pp. 240–241.

44. Ibid., p. 239.

45. Jerome Hall, *General Principles of Criminal Law*, 2nd ed. (Indianapolis: Bobbs-Merrill, 1960), p. 276. For a brief tribute to Hall as the first legal scholar to incorporate social science insights into his work see Donald R. Cressey, "Jerome Hall." *Hastings Law Journal*, 32 (1981): 394–395.

46. Tappan, "Who Is the Criminal?" p. 190.

47. Ibid., p. 101.

48. Vilhelm Aubert, "White-Collar Crime and Social Structure." *American Journal of Sociology*, 58 (1952), p. 264,

49. Ibid., p. 266.

50. Ibid., p. 270.

51. Robert G. Caldwell, "A Re-Examination of the Concept of White-Collar Crime," *Federal Probation*, 22 (March 1958): 30–36.

52. Herbert Edelhertz, *The Nature, Impact and Prosecution of White-Collar Crime* (Washington, DC: Law Enforcement Assistance Administration, US Department of Justice, 1970), pp. 3–4.

53. Ibid., p. 4.

54. Ibid., pp. 19–20.

55. I do not mean this harshly. Herb was a close friend and we published several things together, including a book on crime victim compensation.

56. Miriam S. Saxon, *White-Collar Crime: The Problem and the Federal Response* (Washington, DC: Congressional Research Office, Library of Congress, 1980). See generally Ralph Adam Fine, *The Great Drug Deception: The Shocking Story of MER.29 and the Folks Who Gave You Thalidomide* (New York: Stein and Day, 1972).

57. Peter Applebome, "The Pariah as Client: Bombing Case Rekindles Debate for Lawyers." *New York Times*, April 29, 1995, p. B10. See also Maurice Punch, "Suite Violence: Why Managers Murder and Corporations Kill." *Crime, Law and Social Change*, 33 (2000): 243–280.

58. American Bar Association, *White Collar Crime* (Washington, DC: The Association, 1997), p. 5.

59. *Leocal v. Ashcroft*, 125 S. Ct. 377, 382 (2004). The statute is 18 U.S.C.§16(a).

60. Bureau of Justice Statistics, US Department of Justice, *Dictionary of Criminal Justice Terminology*, 2nd ed. (Washington, DC: Government Printing Office, 1981), p. 215.

61. Harold E. Pepinsky, "From White-Collar Crime to Exploitation: Redefinition of a Field." *Journal of Criminal Law & Criminology*, 65 (1974), p. 226.

62. Ibid., p. 230.

63. Ibid.

64. Michael P. Zucker, *Natural Rights and the New Republicanism* (Princeton, N.J.: Princeton University Press, 1994).

65. Leonard Orland, "Reflections on Corporate Crime: Law in Search of Theory and Scholarship." *American Criminal Law Review*, 17 (1980), p. 503.

66. Ibid., p. 504.

67. Marshall Clinard, Peter Yeager, Jeane Brisette, David Petrashek, and Elizabeth Harris, *Illegal Corporate Behavior* (Washington, DC: US Government Printing Office, 1979). It is noteworthy that when this report appeared in book form, authored by Clinard and Yeager, it had been retitled *Corporate Crime* (New York: Free Press, 1980).

68. Orland, "Reflections on Corporate Crime, p. 506.

69. Sutherland, *White Collar Crime*, p. 125.

70. See Stanton Wheeler, "The Prospects for Large-Scale Collaborative Research: Re-Visiting the Yale White-Collar Crime Research Program." *Law and Social Inquiry*, 18 (1993): 101–113.

71. Kathleen Daly, "Gender and Varieties of White-Collar Crime." *Criminology*, 27 (1989), p. 790.

72. Jane Roberts Chapman, *Economic Realities and the Female Offender* (Lexington, MA: Lexington Books, 1980), p. 68. A historian labeled crimes by the nobility in England during the middle ages as "fur-collar crime." Barbara A. Hanawalt, "Fur-Collar Crime: The Pattern of Crime among Fourteenth-Century Nobility." *Journal of Social History*, 8 (1975): 1–17.

73. Stanton Wheeler, David Weisburd, and Nancy Bode, "Sentencing the White-Collar Offender: Rhetoric and Reality." *American Sociological Review* 47 (1982): 641–659.

74. John Hagan and Patricia Parker, "White-Collar Crime and Punishment: The Class Structure and Legal Sanctioning of Securities Violations." *American Sociological Review* 50 (1987): 302–315.

75. Robert Tillman and Henry N. Pontell, "Is Justice 'Collar Blind'?: Punishing Medicaid Provider Fraud." *Criminology*, 30 (1992): 547–573. See also William K. Black, *The Best Way to Rob a Bank Is to Own One: How Corporate Executives and Politicians Looted the S&L Industry* (Austin: University of Texas Press, 2005).

76. David Weisburd, Elin Waring, and Ellen F. Chayet, *White-Collar Crime and Criminal Careers* (New York: Cambridge University Press, 2001).

77. David Weisburd, Stanton Wheeler, Elin Waring, and Nancy Bode, *Crimes of the Middle Class: White Collar Offenders in the Federal Courts* (New Haven, CT: Yale University Press, 1991), p. 9.

78. "White-Collar Criminals Unmasked," *Harvard Law Review* 105 (1992): 2100. See also David T. Johnson and Richard Leo, "The Yale White-Collar Crime Project: A Review," *Law & Social Inquiry* 18 (1993): 63–99.

79. Ibid., p. 80.

80. Ibid., p. 10.
81. Susan P. Shapiro, "Collaring the Crime, Not the Criminal: Liberating the Concept of White-Collar Crime." *American Sociological Review*, 55 (1990), p. 346.
82. Ibid., p. 363.
83. Ibid., p. 357.
84. Ibid., p. 362. See also Susan P. Shapiro, "Policing Trust." In Clifford P. Shearing and Philip C. Stennings, eds. *Private Policing* (Newbury Park, CA: Sage, 1987), pp. 194–201.
85. David O. Friedrichs, "White Collar Crime and the Definitional Quagmire: A Provisional Solution." *Journal of Human Justice*, 3 (1992), p. 9.
86. James Q. Wilson and Richad Herrnstein, *Crime and Human Nature* (New York: Simon and Schuster, 1985).
87. Edwin H. Sutherland, *Principles of Criminology*, 4th ed. (Philadelphia: J. B. Lippincott, 1947), pp. 5–9.
88. Donald R. Cressey, "Epidemiology and Individual Conduct." *Pacific Sociological Review*, 3 (1960): 47–58.
89. Donald R. Cressey, *Other People's Money: A Study in the Social Psychology of Embezzlement* (Glencoe, IL: Free Press, 1953). See also Cressey, "Application and Verification of the Differential Association Theory." *Journal of Criminal Law, Criminology, and Police Science*, 43 (1952): 43–52.
90. Anthony Harris, "Sex and Theories of Deviance: Toward a Functional Theory of Deviant Type-Scripts." *American Sociology Review*, 42 (1977), p. 8.
91. Solomon Kobrin, "The Conflict of Values in Delinquency Areas." *American Sociological Review*, 16 (1951): 653–661.
92. Travis C. Pratt and Francis Cullen, "The Empirical Status of Gottfredson and Hirschi's General Theory of Crime." *Criminology*, 38 (2000), p. 944. See generally Ross Matsueda, "The Current State of Differential Association Theory." *Crime & Delinquency*, 34 (1988): 277–306.
93. John B. Mays, *Crime and Social Structure* (London: Faber and Faber, 1963), p. 67.
94. Nigel Walker, *Crime and Punishment in Britain* (Edinburgh: University Press, 1965), p. 95. See generally Walker, *A Man Without Loyalties: A Penologist's Afterthoughts* (Chichester: Barry Rose Law Publishers, 2003).
95. Leon Radzinowicz, *Ideology and Crime* (New York: Columbia University Press, 1966), p. 81.
96. John Braithwaite, Crime, Shame and Reintegration (Cambridge, England: Cambridge University Press, 1989), 37–38. An effort to add some concrete reinforcement in the theory appears in Ross L. Matsueda, "The Current State of Differential Association Theory," *Crime & Delinquency* 34 (1988): 277–306.
97. James W. Coleman, "Toward an Integrated Theory of White-Collar Crime." *American Journal of Sociology*, 93 (1987), p. 408. See also Coleman, "The

Theory of White-Collar Crime: From Sutherland to the 1990s." In Kip Schlegel and David Weisburd, eds., *White-Collar Crime Reconsidered* (Boston: Northeastern University Press, 1992), pp. 53–77.

98. Robert F. Meier and Gilbert Geis, "The White-Collar Offender." In Hans Toch, ed., *Psychology of Crime and Criminal Justice* (New York: Holt, Rinehart and Winston, 1979), p. 441.

99. Peter C. Whybrow, *American Mania: When More Is Not Enough* (New York: W. W. Norton, 2005).

100. Coleman, "Toward and Integrated Theory," p. 409.

101. James D. Orcott, "Differential Association and Marijuana Use: A Closer Look at Sutherland (With a Little Help from Becker). *Criminology*, 25 (1987): 341–358.

102. Coleman, "Toward an Integrated Theory," p. 424.

103. Michael Gottfredson and Travis Hirschi, *A General Theory of Crime* (Stanford, CA: Stanford University Press, 1990), p. 171.

104. Ibid., p. xiv.

105. Ibid., p. 90.

106. Ibid., pp. 269–270,

107. Travis Hirschi and Michael Gottfredson, "Causes of White-Collar Crime." *Criminology*, 25 (1987), p. 959.

108. Travis Hirschi and Michael Gottfredson, "Commentary: Testing the General Theory of Crime." *Journal of Research in Crime and Delinquency*, 30 (1993), p. 82.

109. Hirschi and Gottfredson, "Causes of White-Collar Crime," p. 950; see also Hirschi and Gottfredson, "The Significance of White-Collar Crime for a General Theory of Crime." *Criminology*, 27 (1989): 359–371.

110. Darell Steffensmeier, "On the Causes of 'White-Collar Crime': An Assessment of Hirschi and Gottfredson's Claims." *Criminology*, 27 (1989): 345–358.

111. Gottfredson and Hirschi, *A General Theory*, p. 189.

112. See Steffensmeier, "On the Causes of 'White-Collar Crime'; Michael L. Benson and Elizabeth Moore, "Are White-Collar and Common Offenders the Same?: An Empirical and Theoretical Critique of a Recently Proposed General Theory of Crime." *Journal of Research in Crime and Delinquency*, 29 (1992): 251–272; Gary E. Reed and Peter C. Yeager, "Organizational Offending and Neo-Classical Criminology: Challenging the Reach of a General Theory of Crime." *Criminology* 34 (1996): 357–382.

113. James B. Stewart, *Den of Thieves* (New York: Simon and Schuster, 1991).

114. Dennis B. Levine and William Hoffer. *Inside Out: An Insider's Account of Wall Street* (New York: G. P. Putnam's, 1991).

115. Jesse Kornbluth, *Highly Confident: The Crime and Punishment of Michael Milken* (New York: Morrow, 1992).

116. Kenneth Polk, "Review of *A General Theory of Crime.*" *Crime and Delinquency* 37 (1991), p. 578.

117. Gottfredson and Hirschi, *A General Theory of Crime*, p. 40.
118. Robert Tillman and Henry N. Pontell, "Organizations and Fraud in the Savings and Loan Industry." *Social Forces*, 73 (1995), p. 1459.
119. Wilson and Herrnstein, *Crime and Human Nature*, pp. 21–22.
120. Gottfredson and Hirschi, *A General Theory of Crime*, p. 116.
121. Jack Katz, *Seductions of Crime: Moral and Sensual Attractions in Doing Evil* (New York: Basic Books, 1988), p. 319.
122. Neal Shove and Andy Hochstetler, *Choosing White-Collar Crime* (New York: Cambridge University Press, 2006), 1.
123. Derek B. Cornish and Ronald V. Clarke, *The Reasoning Criminal: Rational Choice Perspective on Offending* (New York: Springer-Verlag, 1986), p. 1.
124. President's Commission on Law Enforcement and Administration of Justice, *Assessment Task Force Report* (Washington, DC: Government Printing Office, 1967), p. 1.
125. Robert A. Nisbet, *Makers of Modern Science: Emile Durkheim* (Englewood Cliffs, NJ: Prentice Hall, 1965), p. 39.

INDEX